French Bulldog

A guide to selection, care, nutrition, rearing, training,

health, breeding, sports and play.

This book is an essential for every French Bulldog owner

or anyone considering a French Bulldog as a pet.

© 2011 About Pets bv
P.O. Box 26, 9989 ZG Warffum, the Netherlands
www.aboutpets.info
E-mail: management@aboutpets.info

ISBN: 978-90-5821-849-0
First edition 2011

Photos: About Pets photography team

Breed information: Maya Brünner
Acknowledgements:
Photos: Conny van Randeraad, Fred and Belinda, Nico and Lisette van Braak, José
Luijten van der Zwaan, Heiko and Sabine Lorenzs
Anatomic illustrations: Hill's
Graphs: Courtesy of Royal Canin

Contents

Foreword

This book is an essential for every French Bulldog owner or anyone considering the breed as a pet. It traces the ancestry of the French Bulldog, explores the breed standard and some pros and cons of buying the breed. There is also important advice on feeding, as well as information on initial training and an introduction to reproduction. Finally, this book includes sections on day-to-day care, health and some breed-specific ailments.

About Pets

In general

These small, molossian dogs are really adoring human beings and they can go along very well with other dogs. The French Bulldog is often described as "a clown in the cloak of a philosopher". The French Bulldog is a medium to small sized companion dog and it is bred in three colours: brindle, pied and fawn. It has a short coat that is easy to keep clean. It is a small and muscular breed with heavy bone structure, a short face and its trademark are its "bat" ears. The French Bulldog has an affectionate disposition, it is very intelligent and it always is ready for fun. Furthermore the French Bulldog is fond of children.

This breed cannot be kept in a kennel, it needs a lot of love, affection and companion from its family. It has a jolly and engaging personality and is very vivacious. The Frenchie (as it is often called) is neither a boisterous nor a noisy dog. The French Bulldog will happily live in a house or in a flat as an integral part of its family. It has a strong desire to please and really needs to be a part of the family.

The French Bulldog is a very sensitive dog that knows when its family is in a good mood or in a bad mood. It is not able to stand a loud voice of its master.

It adapts itself easily to different environments, which makes it also a perfect dog for elder people. In case someone wants to have more than one dog, another molossian breed as its companion should be an excellent choice. The company of its family is of the utmost importance to this little clown that does not like to be left alone. It is a real family-dog.

Sometimes the French Bulldog can be very possessive of its owner and then it does not want to share him/her. A kind but firm rearing may be necessary with some Frenchies as they sometimes have to be reminded who is its boss.

The French Bulldog enjoys playing with children. However children and dogs should never be left alone together, an adult supervisor should always be with them.

The Frenchie does not need long walks, it prefers to play but it also enjoys a stroll with its owner. This breed is not a guard dog, however it certainly will warn its family, when a stranger approaches the house. Some Frenchies will even defend their property and owners. The French Bulldog will not start fights with other dog breeds, however when it is challenged it certainly is not afraid. Because of its 'flat face', other dog breeds do not always like the French Bulldog.

Origins

3800 years BC the first Molossian dogs were taken from the Tibetan Highlands by Sumerians. They settled between Tigris and the Euphrates. The Greeks called this territory Mesopotamia, the land between two rivers.
350 years BC Alexander the Great entered into a combat with the Mesopotamians and the Persians, he met an army that was equipped with fighting dogs. Of course, the dogs that were captured were taken to Greece, these dogs were Molossian Dogs.
Molossos was a place in Greece, where Alexander the Great used to have his kennels for breeding these fighting dogs. This place Molossos underlies the name "Molossian Dog".

Another version about the Molossian dogs concerns a tribe in Hellas, the old Greece. This tribe themselves was called Molossian. In the northwest mountain region they had their sheep herded by their dogs. The Phoenicians (originating from the present Lebanon) were trading with the present Europe. In that way the dogs from the Sumerians finally arrived on our coastal regions.

The Indo-Germanic people took Molossian look alike dogs with them from the Far East.

In the end it were the Englishmen that have imported many dogs as a consequence of being a maritime country and their colonial power. Meanwhile the Molossian Dog is an extinct breed. It is regarded as the ancestor of the present English Mastiff Dog, the Dogue the Bordeaux and the Neapolitan Mastiff. The English Bulldog is seen as the direct ancestor of the French Bulldog. In 1630 the English Bulldog is mentioned as a breed for the first time.

History

In spite of its name, the French Bulldog is believed to be at least partly of British origin. It is supposed to be a descendant of the Toy Bulldog, which was bred in Great Britain during the 19th century.

Around the year 1820 it was no longer necessary, to have bull-baiting dogs, because the "sport bull baiting" was prohibited.

The dogs that had been used for this type of sport were crossbred with other dogs, maybe with the intention to breed dogs that were suitable to keep as a pet. Small dogs were also used to cross with this breed. Because no written history could be found, we have to guess what happened. Maybe even small terriers were used in breeding. It is also said, that small dogs with erect ears were found in the litters from those breeders. Those breeders were not satisfied with that and tried to sell those dogs to craftsmen. These small dogs, the toy-bulldogs, were highly appreciated by the lace-makers from Nottingham.
The ears of the former Bull Baiting dogs used to be tip-ears, so it could be possible as well that the erect ears are a result of using terriers in cross-breeding.

During the 19th century, in Nottingham (U.K.), the lace-makers were selectively breeding the early bulldog for a downsized or "toy" bulldog. They wanted to create a lap pet. Because of the industrial revolution, the lace-makers from the Midlands lost their jobs and they went to work in France. Of course they took their small Bulldogs with them and soon these small dogs became very popular in France. In France they settled mainly in Normandy, where the small dogs were used as a ratter and as a pet in the families.

It is also believed, that these dogs were bred with short-faced bull-baiting dogs that were originating from other European countries. Another theory is, that the dogs that were taken to France, very soon become popular and on a regular base were crossbred with the Griffon Belge and the Pug.

We should also take into account that in those days Paris was the fashion centre of the world. Everything coming from Paris was said to be beautiful and people wanted to have it. The dog authority from those days, Paul Megnin, assumed that the butchers who were settled near "Les Halles" (the market place) in Paris used to have Molossian Dogs for ages. In 1870 the Terrier Boules made their entry into this environment. In those days, the ears were cropped and the dogs were used as rattlers. A small dog is very suitable for this kind of job.

The real success of the breed started in 1880, when the people who had an interest in these dogs, came together regularly. This resulted in keeping up a register with the names of these dogs from 1885 onwards. As early as 1887, a French Bulldog was exhibited on a dog show, at that moment it already had the name "French Bulldog". From that moment on, everything went fast. In 1888 Marcel Roger founded the breeding club and the first breed standard was drawn up.

In 1898, the breed was also accepted by the Société Centrale Canine of France and it was that organisation that proposed Gordon Bennet, who had founded the French Bulldog Lovers' Club, and Marcel Roger from the Breeding club to start to work together. This resulted in the foundation of the "Bouledogeu Club de France" with Menans de Corre as its president and Gordon Bennet as its vice president.
In 1898 the breed was officially recognized thanks to the effort of Baron Caravon de la Tour. A famous dog from those days was "Rabot de Beauborg".

The French Bulldog used to be the dog for the common people. Many women of easy virtue have been taken on a picture together with their "Bouledogues Français", as is shown on ancient, French picture postcards. Pretty soon the French Bulldog became popular within the European world of entertainment. In 1887, in his painting "Le Marchand des Marrons" (the chestnut costermonger) Toulouse Lautrec painted some French Bulldogs. King Edward VII had a French Bulldog and on portraits of the Russian czar family French Bulldogs can very often be seen. When in 1991 the remains of the Romanovs (the czar family) were excavated, the skeleton of a terrier like dog was found as well. This must have been the skeleton of Ortino, the French Bulldog of daughter Tatiana. She got this dog as a present on 12th October 1914, the whole family was charmed of Ortina and very soon a second French Bulldog named Bille arrived.
These dogs were allowed to do whatever they wanted to do, and they rushed behind each other within the palace. Tatiana wrote every day in her diary about her dog and when the Romanovs were picked up during the revolution in 1917, she took Ortino with her. So it is almost for sure, that it was the skeleton of Ortino. During the official burial of the remains of the Romanovs, the skeleton of Ortino was buried as well.

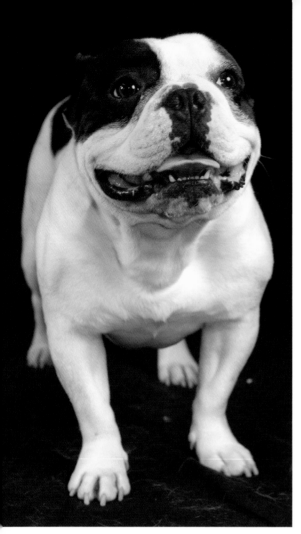

The bat ears and the short tail were characteristic features of this new breed that became known as the "French Bulldog" in late 1800. The French name is "Bouledogue Français". This type of dogs went to England, where they were exhibited on a dog show around 1900. In Great Britain the French Bulldog Club was established in 1903.

In the early days of breeding in Europe, everybody preferred the rose ear. The Americans preferred the bat ear. This controversy over type resulted in the formation of the French Bulldog Club of America. In 1898 fanciers gave a specialty show in the ballroom of the Waldorf-Astoria .

The breed standard has been modified in 1931, 1932 and in 1948.
In 1986 the standard was reformulated by H.F. Reant and R. Triquet (F.C.I. publication 1987). In 1994, the standard was modified again by the committee of the Club of the French Bulldog with the collaboration of R. Triquet.

The ears of the French Bulldog occupied breeders and owners during a long period of time. They wonder, when exactly the erect ears came into being.

What is for sure is the fact that the Americans founded the first breed-club "The French Bulldog club" and that it was the influence of this breed-club that took care of the acceptance that the erect bat ears were the correct ears and not the rose ears. Both types of ears could be found on the heads of the French Bulldogs during many years.

Character
The French Bulldog is a sociable, lively, playful, sporty and keen little dog. It is extremely affectionate towards its masters and the children.

Appearance
The French Bulldog is a typical small size Molossian Dog. For its small size, the French Bulldog is a powerful dog.
The dog is short and compact in all its proportions. It has a smooth coated and a short face with a snub nose.
The bat ears and the naturally short tail are characteristic features.
The French Bulldog must have the appearance of an active animal that is intelligent and very muscular. The dog is compact build with a solid bone structure.

UK Kennel Club and its breed standards

What does the UK Kennel Club do?

To say it in their own words: "The Kennel Club is committed to developing and supporting a nation of responsible dog owners. As well as organising events and campaigns to help dog owners meet their responsibilities, the Kennel Club also produces a range of literature to assist the dog owning public."

What is the use of a Breed Standard?

The Kennel Club explains that "the basis of breed shows is the judging of dogs against the 'Breed Standard', which is the prescribed blueprint of the particular breed of dog. For all licensed breed shows, the Kennel Club Breed Standards must be used for the judging of dogs."

More about the UK Kennel Club Breed Standards:

"The Breed Standards are owned by the Kennel Club, and all changes are subject to approval by the Kennel Club General Committee. New Breed Standards, for newly recognised breeds, are drawn up once the breed has become sufficiently established within the UK. Careful research is conducted into the historical background, health and temperament of any new breed before Kennel Club recognition is granted. The Kennel Club currently recognises 210 breeds. Upon recognition, breeds are placed on the Imported Breed Register until they are deemed eligible for transferral to the Breed Register".

A standard provides a guideline for breeders and judges. It is used as an ideal that dogs of each breed can be compared to in order to assess the quality of their breeding - breeders strive to meet this standard in their dogs. In some breeds, dogs have been bred that already reach this standard, other breeds have a long way to go. There is a list of defects for each breed, these can be serious defects that disqualify the dog, in which case it will be excluded from breeding. Permitted defects are not serious, but do cost points in a show. A standard has been developed for all breeds recognised by the FCI (Fédération Cynologique Internationale).

More about the FCI

The Fédération Cynologique Internationale is the World Canine Organisation. The FCI has 86 members all over the world and contract partners (one member per country); each country issues its own pedigrees and trains its own judges. The FCI makes sure that the pedigrees and judges are mutually recognised by all the FCI members. The FCI is the worldwide umbrella organisation in the dog world. The officially approved breed associations of the member countries provide translations of the breed standard.

The FCI recognises 339 breeds (2010), and each breed is the 'property' of a specific country. The country, which is 'owner' of the breed, writes the standard - a description of the ideal type - of this breed in co-operation with the Standards and Scientific Commissions of the FCI. The translation and updating are carried out by the FCI. The breed-standards are incredibly important as they act as the reference for judges when they judge dogs in shows held in the FCI member countries.

The breed-standard is also THE reference that assists the breeders in their attempt to produce top-quality dogs.

The UK Kennel Club Breed Standard of the French Bulldog

General Appearance. Sturdy, compact, solid, small dog with good bone, short, smooth coat. No point exaggerated, balance essential. Dogs showing respiratory distress highly undesirable.

Characteristics. Full of courage, yet with clown-like qualities. Bat ears and short tail characteristic features of the breed.

Temperament. Vivacious, deeply affectionate, intelligent.

Head and Skull. Head square in appearance and in proportion to dog's size. Skull nearly flat between ears, domed forehead. The skin covering the skull and forehead should be supple enough to allow fine wrinkling when the dog is alert. Well-defined muzzle, broad, deep and set back, muscles of cheeks well developed. Stop well defined. Lower jaw deep, square, broad, slightly undershot and turned up. Nose black and wide, relatively short, with open nostrils and line between well defined. Lips black, thick, meeting each other in centre, completely hiding teeth. Upper lip covers lower on each side with plenty of cushion, never so exaggerated as to hang too much below level of lower jaw.

Eyes. Preferably dark and matching. Moderate size, round, neither sunken nor prominent, showing no white when looking straight forward; set relatively wide apart and on same level as the stop.

Ears. 'Bat ears', of medium size, wide at base, rounded at top; set high, carried upright and parallel, a sufficient width of skull preventing them being too close together; skin soft and fine, orifice as seen from the front, showing entirely. The opening to the ear canal should be wide and open.

Mouth. Slightly undershot. Teeth sound and regular, but not visible when the mouth is closed. Tongue must not protrude.

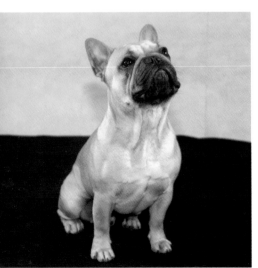

Neck. Powerful, well arched and thick, of moderate length.

Forequarters. Legs set wide apart, straight boned, strong, muscular and short.

Body. Cobby, muscular and well rounded with deep wide brisket and ribs well sprung. Strong, gently roached back. Good 'cut up'. The body while broader at the shoulders should narrow slightly beyond the ribs to give definition to the relatively short, thick, strong, muscular loin.

Hindquarters. Legs strong, muscular and relatively longer than forelegs with moderate angulations. Absolute soundness essential. Hocks well let down.

Feet. Small, compact and placed in continuation of line of leg, with absolutely sound pasterns. Hind feet rather longer than the forefeet.
Toes compact; well knuckled; nails short, thick and preferably black.

Tail. Undocked, short, set low, thick at root, tapering quickly towards tip, preferably straight and long enough to cover anus, never curling over back nor carried gaily.

Gait/Movement. Free and flowing. Soundness of movement of the utmost importance.

Coat. Texture fine, smooth, lustrous, short and close.

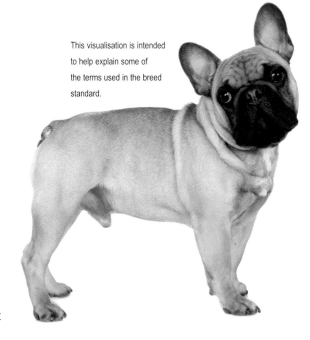

This visualisation is intended to help explain some of the terms used in the breed standard.

Colour. Brindle, pied or fawn. Tan, mouse and grey/blue highly undesirable.
Brindle: a mixture of black and coloured hairs. May contain white provided brindle predominates.
Pied: white predominates over brindle.
Whites are classified with pieds for show purposes; but their eyelashes and eye rims should be black. In pieds the white should be clear with definite brindle patches and no ticking or black spots.
Fawn: may contain brindle hairs but must have black eye lashes and eye rims.

Size. Ideal weight: dogs: 12.5 kg (28 lbs); bitches: 11 kg (24 lbs). Soundness not to be sacrificed to smallness.

Faults. Any departure from the foregoing points should be considered a fault and the seriousness with which the fault should be regarded should be in exact proportion to its degree and its effect upon the health and welfare of the dog.

Note. Male animals should have two apparently normal testicles fully descended into the scrotum.

Reproduced by courtesy of the UK Kennel Club, October 2009

More about the American Kennel Club
The American Kennel Club (A.K.C.) is the national kennel organisation of the United States. This organisation was already founded in 1884. The A.K.C. is not a member of the F.C.I.

The American Kennel Club is the national organisation for the registration of purebred dogs and they promote the sport of purebred dogs.

Apart from that the A.K.C. also promotes breeding purebred dogs for type and function. Furthermore the A.K.C. promotes responsible dog ownership and tries to protect the rights of all dog owners.
The A.K.C. tries to protect the health and well being of dogs.

The breed standards of the A.K.C. can differ from the F.C.I. and UK breed standards. Between the F.C.I. and the A.K.C. exists a letter of understanding in which several cooperation agreements are laid down.
Both organisations share the same common goals of promoting and protecting purebred dogs.

The American Kennel Club Breed Standard for the French Bulldog

General Appearance
The French Bulldog has the appearance of an active, intelligent, muscular dog of heavy bone, smooth coat, compactly built, and of medium or small structure. Expression alert, curious, and interested. Any alteration other than removal of dewclaws is considered mutilation and is a disqualification.
Proportion and Symmetry: All points are well distributed and bear good relation one to the other; no feature being in such prominence from either excess or lack of quality that the animal appears poorly proportioned.

Influence of Sex
In comparing specimens of different sex, due allowance is to be made in favour of bitches, which do not bear the characteristics of the breed to the same marked degree as do the dogs.

Size, Proportion, Substance
Weight not to exceed 28 pounds; over 28 pounds is a disqualification. Proportion: Distance from withers to ground in good relation to distance from withers to onset of tail, so that animal appears compact, well balanced and in good proportion. Substance: Muscular, heavy bone.

Head
Head large and square. *Eyes* dark in colour, wide apart, set low down in the skull, as far from the ears as possible, round in form, of moderate size, neither sunken nor bulging. In lighter coloured dogs, lighter coloured eyes are acceptable. No haw and no white of the eye showing when looking forward. *Ears* Known as the bat ear, broad at the base, elongated, with round top, set high on the head but not too close together, and carried erect with the orifice to the front. The leather of the ear fine and soft. Other than bat ears is a disqualification. The *top of the skull* flat between the ears; the *forehead* is not flat but slightly rounded. The *muzzle broad*, deep and well laid back; the *muscles of the cheeks* well developed. The *stop* well defined, causing a hollow groove between the eyes with heavy wrinkles forming a soft roll over the extremely short nose; *nostrils broad* with a well defined line between them. *Nose* black. Nose other than black is a disqualification, except in the case of the lighter coloured dogs, where a lighter coloured nose is acceptable but not desirable. *Flews* black, thick and broad, hanging over the lower jaw at

the sides, meeting the under-lip in front and covering the teeth, which are not seen when the mouth is closed. The *under-jaw* is deep, square, broad, undershot and well turned up.

Neck, Top-line, Body
The *neck* is thick and well arched with loose skin at the throat. The *back* is a roach back with a slight fall close behind the shoulders; strong and short, broad at the shoulders and narrowing at the loins. The *body* is short and well rounded. The *chest* is broad, deep, and full; well ribbed with the belly tucked up. The *tail* is either straight or screwed (but not curly), short, hung low, thick root and fine tip; carried low in repose.

Forequarters
Forelegs are short, stout, straight, muscular and set wide apart. *Dewclaws* may be removed. *Feet* are moderate in size, compact and firmly set. *Toes* compact, well split up, with high knuckles and short stubby nails.

Hindquarters
Hind legs are strong and muscular, longer than the forelegs, so as to elevate the loins

above the shoulders. *Hocks* well let down. *Feet* are moderate in size, compact and firmly set. *Toes* compact, well split up, with high knuckles and short stubby nails; *hind feet* slightly longer than forefeet.

Coat
Coat is moderately fine, brilliant, short and smooth. *Skin* is soft and loose, especially at the head and shoulders, forming wrinkles.

Colour
Acceptable colours - All brindle, fawn, white, brindle and white, and any colour except those, which constitute disqualification. All colours are acceptable with the exception of solid black, mouse, liver, black and tan, black and white, and white with black, which are disqualifications. Black means black without a trace of brindle.

Gait
Correct gait is double tracking with reach and drive; the action is unrestrained, free and vigorous.

Temperament
Well behaved, adaptable, and comfortable companions with an affectionate nature and even disposition; generally active, alert, and playful, but not unduly boisterous.

Disqualifications
Any alteration other than removal of dewclaws.
Over 28 pounds in weight.
Other than bat ears.
Nose other than black, except in the case of lighter coloured dogs, where a lighter coloured nose is acceptable.
Solid black, mouse, liver, black and tan, black and white, and white with black.
Black means black without a trace of brindle.

Produced by courtesy of the American Kennel Club, July 1991

Purchase

If, after careful consideration, you have decided to buy a French Bulldog there are a number of options available to you. Do you want a puppy or an adult dog? Should it be a male or female?
One of the biggest questions that will arise, of course, is where you should buy your dog. Should you buy it privately or from a reliable breeder? For your own and the animal's sake, a few things should be decided in advance. After all, you want a dog that suits your situation and lifestyle.

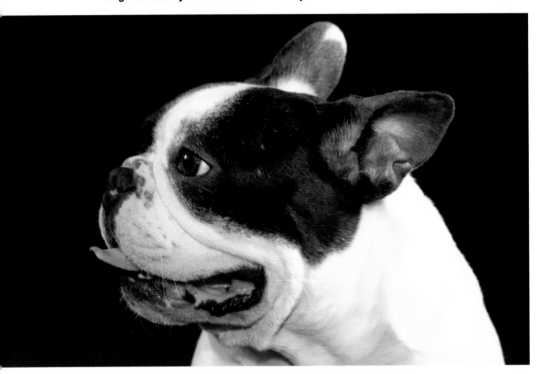

Pros and cons of the French Bulldog

The French Bulldogs is a companion dog that cannot be kept in a kennel. What they really need is human love and affection. Without the companionship of the members of their family they will not thrive. This breed has a strong desire to please and most important for the French Bulldog is to be part of its family. The main function of a French Bulldog is to be a lap dog!

A French Bulldog is a really intelligent dog with a mischievous side and it is well known for its clownish behaviour. Sometimes the breed will become possessive towards its owner and does not want to share him/her with another dog, a child or even its partner. In this case a strict but kind rearing will be needed, because even a Frenchie has to learn to remember who is the leader of the pack!

A French Bulldog loves to play with children, however children and dogs should never be left alone without the supervision of an adult. This rule has to be applied to all dogs, even to all animals.

It is not necessary to take a French Bulldog out for longer walks. The Frenchie prefers to play, nevertheless when its owner wants to make a walk in the area, the Frenchie enjoys being out together with its master. The best way to exercise your French Bulldog is: short bursts of high-energy activity, followed by longer periods of rest and relaxation.

The French Bulldog is not a guard dog, however it will warn its family when a stranger is coming to its house. Some Frenchies even will defend their property and owners.

The Frenchie is an easygoing dog towards other dogs, however because of its 'flat face' other dog breeds do not always like the French Bulldog. In case it will be challenged by another dog, it will not back down (this is an inheritance from its ancestors the Molossian Dogs).

A French Bulldog will be house trained rather quickly. However when it is raining, they do not want to go outside, so get them used to that in an early age.

Because of the way a French Bulldog is built, it very often is not able to swim, and as its owner you have to protect him against the risks of drowning in great pools, ponds or rivers.

The French Bulldog needs a varied diet, because they get bored with eating the same food all the time. Very often they prefer the food that its owner is eating. However never allow your Frenchie to eat food for people. Two smaller meals of a high quality dog food per day are preferable to one large meal. *See the chapter about "Food"*.
The coat of a French Bulldog is easy to groom.

A French Bulldog is an independent thinker that means that this breed often is not the best breed in obedience competitions. Apart from that it is not recommended to use the Frenchie for agility activities.

Although many French Bulldogs can reach a high age, up to 13 and 14 years, sometimes-spinal abnormalities can cause problems. Elongated soft palate and its narrow airways can cause breathing problems. Within the breed sometimes allergies and skins problems can occur. Its ears and facial wrinkles need to be cleaned regularly, as well as the area under its tail. When they get older, the breed can be susceptible to eye ulcers. *More about this in the chapter "Health".*

Most important:
The most serious and even life-threatening situation for a French Bulldog is, when it is left alone in a car or when it is separated from its owner in a stressful situation. The combination of stress and heat can be fatal for your French Bulldog.

Male or female?
Whether you buy a male or a female is mainly a question of personal preference. Both can grow up to become attractive and well behaved members of the family. As far as working capacity is concerned, there is no difference between a dog and a bitch.

Males sometimes appear to be more self-assured and can display dominant behaviour, trying to play boss over other dogs, especially over other males, and, if they get the chance, over humans too. In the wild the most dominant dog (or wolf) was always the leader of the pack - and in most cases this was a male.
It is essential, in order to establish a good relationship between dog and owner, that the dog understands from the outset that you are the leader of the pack. This demands an understanding yet consistent upbringing.

Bitches usually become fertile (go on heat) between eight and twelve months. This happens twice a year and lasts two to three weeks. During the fertile period, especially during the second half of the season, the female will try to go out in search of a male to mate with. It is essential that you take precautions to prevent unwanted additions to the family.

A male will display more masculine behaviour once he becomes sexually mature. He will make clear to other dogs which territory is his by urinating frequently and in as many places as possible. He will also be very difficult to confine when there is a bitch in season in the area.
However, as far as general care is concerned, there is little difference between male and female on a daily basis

A puppy test is good way of determining what kind of character a young dog will develop. During this test you will usually notice that a dog is more dominant than a bitch; it is also often possible to quickly recognise the bossy, the adventurous and the cautious characters. Visit the litter a couple of times early on and try to pick a puppy that suits your own personality. A dominant dog, for instance, needs a strong hand as it will often try and test its boundaries. You must regularly make it clear who's the boss, and ensure that he understands he must obey all the members of the family.

Puppy or adult dog?

After you have decided you want a male or female, the question arises as to whether it should be a puppy or an adult dog?

Of course, it is great having a sweet little puppy in the house, but training a young dog requires a lot of time. In the first year it learns more than during the rest of its life. This is the period when the foundations are laid for fundamental training such as house-training, obedience and social behaviour. You should be prepared to devote a lot of time to training and caring for your puppy - especially in the first few months.

A puppy will no doubt leave a trail of destruction in its wake for the first few months, this will usually cost you a number of rolls of wallpaper, some good shoes and a few socks, in the worst case scenario you'll be left with some chewed furniture - though some puppies even manage to tear curtains from their rails! With some basic training this 'vandalism' will quickly disappear as your puppy grows.

The greatest advantage of a puppy is of course, that you can train it in your own way. The training a dog gets or does not get is a major influence on its whole character.

A puppy requires a good deal of time and energy, but ultimately, you will have a significant influence on its character and behaviour, and will hopefully end up with a dog that suits you and your lifestyle.

Choosing an adult French Bulldog is an option if training a puppy does not appeal to you. However, it is important to recognize that an older dog will still require a significant amount of input from you. An adult French Bulldog is also likely to have developed its own habits, traits and characteristics that you will have to accept if you decide to choose an older dog. Equally, it will have probably grown used to a certain type of lifestyle, which you may struggle to adapt to.

Integrating an adult dog into a household with an existing dog can be tricky, and it is essential you handle this introduction with sensitivity. Both dogs will need time to adjust and establish their natural hierarchy.

If you are interested in an adult French Bulldog you may want to consider rehoming a rescue dog. Most rescue dogs are older dogs in need of a new home through no fault of their own (e.g. a family breakdown or bereavement). However, it is important to be aware that you may experience some difficulties as you and the dog adjust to each other. French Bulldogs are incredibly loyal to their owner and the loss of an owner can be devastating to a loving and devoted dog. As the new owner you must give the dog time and remain gentle and patient until you gain his love and trust. With experience and patience adopting a rescue dog is still a major task, as you may need to correct behavioural issues. Owning any dog is a pleasure for both owner and dog if you can establish a sound relationship.

Adopting a rescued French Bulldog is by no means the easy option and you must be prepared to be vetted by the organization to ensure you are the right match for the dog in question. Most rescue centers will also ask for a donation to help cover the cost of caring for the dog - so it is not always the cheapest option either!

Two dogs?

Having two or more dogs can be great fun for both humans and dogs alike. As pack animals dogs really enjoy each other's company. If you are sure you want two young dogs, it is best not to buy them at the same time. Training a dog and establishing the bond between you and him takes time, and you need to give a lot of attention to the dog in this phase - two puppies in the house means you have to divide your attention. Equally, there is a chance that they will focus on one another rather than on their owner.

It is best to buy a second pup when the first is an adult; two adult dogs can happily be brought into the household together and introducing a puppy when the first dog has matured often has a positive effect on the older dog. The influence of the puppy seems almost to give it a second puppyhood and the older dog, if it has been well trained, can help with the socialisation of the puppy, as young dogs like to imitate the behaviour of their elders. However it is important you divide your attention equally between both dogs. Take the puppy out alone at least once per day during the first eighteen months, and ensure both dogs get enough peace and quiet. You may have to physically separate French Bulldog after a romp, as they never tire of playing together!

The combination of an unneutered male and female also needs special attention as if you do not plan to breed with your dogs, you must take precautionary measures to prevent them mating when the bitch is in season. Spaying the bitch or neutering the male is essential if you are keeping a French Bulldog as a pet.

In case someone wants to have more than one dog, another molossian dog-breed as a companion for the French Bulldog would be an excellent choice.

The French Bulldog and children

Dogs and children can be fantastic playmates, and children can learn important lessons in developing respect and a sense of responsibility through caring for a dog, or other pet. You can encourage this by including your child in the dog's day-to-day care. It is essential that the child understands that a dog is a living being and not a toy, as even the sweetest dog will express its unhappiness if it is being annoyed, and can become frightened, timid and even aggressive. Look for ways the child can play with the dog - games like hide-and-seek (where the child hides and the dog has to find it) are great in establishing a healthy fun-filled relationship between dog and child. While most dogs love playing with children, they do need quiet 'down' time where they are left in peace, and it is essential that you and your children learn to recognise and accept when your dog has had enough.

It can be helpful to create a quiet place for your dog to retreat to in the house when it wants some space - a crate or an indoor kennel can be useful here - especially when the dog is still growing and needs regular periods of rest.

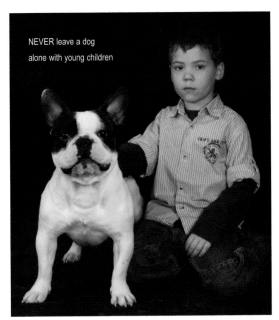
NEVER leave a dog alone with young children

You must bear in mind that some French Bulldogs are fanatical game players and may sometimes snap at a hand, just as at a ball or another toy. They can also jump high and hard in their over-enthusiasm, and you must then really try to calm the dog down.

A young French Bulldog with its limitless energy often will not know when to stop, and you must usually pick the moment when the game is over. A cage or an indoor kennel can be useful here, because a dog needs regular periods of rest for its growth.

The arrival of a baby can also create huge changes in the life of your dog. Before the birth you can help the dog get acquainted with the new situation by letting him sniff the new things in the house. When the baby has arrived involve the dog as much as possible in everyday life, but make sure it gets plenty of attention too.

NEVER leave a dog alone with young children. Crawling infants sometimes make unexpected movements, which can easily frighten a dog. Infants are hugely curious, and may irritate the dog by pulling his tail or invading his space while he is sleeping. Dogs, like all animals, are unpredictable, and even the most mild-mannered dog can instinctively defend itself when if it feels threatened.

A French Bulldog and cats

Contrary to popular belief dogs and cats can coexist quite happily. It is important that you take the time to gently introduce a new puppy to the family cat. As long you ensure the cat has safe places to escape to, and separate places to eat and sleep, they should get along fine.

Many dogs will initially attempt to chase cats, and it is essential you stop this immediately, before it becomes a habit. As their body language is quite different, they need to learn from their experience. For example, a dog lying on its back is submissive. A cat lying on its back is not at all submissive, but makes sure that it has its best weapons of defence, i.e. its claws, at its disposal. However, dogs and cats have one thing in common: they growl when they are angry, and both animals understand this.
As far as nutrients are concerned, Dogs and cats must not share each other's food considering the nutrients. Dog food lacks a sufficient level of taurine, which is essential for cats. Dogs and cats must also not share a food bowl, as a dog will not tolerate another animal sharing its bowl. A persistent kitten might therefore get a serious ticking off from your dog. Playing together is fine, but you must prevent your pets eating together.

Some dogs (this is not a characteristic of any particular breed) love to eat cat faeces (coprophagia). To prevent your dog eating from the cat litter, place the litter box in another room, where only your cat has access, or place the litter box between two pieces of furniture to prevent your dog gaining access.

Where to buy your French Bulldog

The French Bulldog is a popular breed, so there is enough choice. In general it is advisable to be extremely wary of puppies advertised in local papers. These may well be bred by so called 'puppy farmers' who breed for purely financial reasons and give little thought to the quality of the animals they are breeding from. Puppy farmers can rarely produce evidence for the recommended health checks and the bitch is often bred from season after season. This will continue until she is unable to produce any more litters, where upon she will be discarded - with little thought to her quality of life. Equally, puppies reared in this way can be of questionable temperament, and you will generally be unable to meet the parents of the litter. Puppy farmers will often register the litter with the Kennel Club to make the puppies more saleable. Registration itself does not guarantee the legitimacy of the breeder and it is not a benchmark of quality. Buying a puppy from this type of breeder is a huge gamble and it is strongly advised you steer clear from anyone breeding dogs in this way.

Fortunately there are enough responsible breeders with a good reputation. Ask if the breeder is prepared to help you after you have bought your French Bulldog and to help you find solutions to questions or problems that may arise later on. Also, reputable breeders are aware of possible health disorders that are specific to French Bulldogs and the measures they may have taken in their breeding lines.

Breeders who are members of the association must meet its breeding rules. Any breeder that does not stick to these strict conditions is expelled. The UK Kennel Club recently started a kind of health project for its dog breeds: "FIT FOR FUNCTION - FIT FOR LIFE". The French Bulldog Club of England has a Health Scheme, in which they a.o. intend to develop further the Accredited Breeder Scheme.

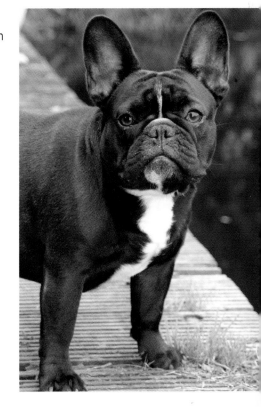

At this moment, there is no recognised health testing in the UK for the French Bulldog. However, the French Bulldog Club of England offers support to its members concerning: heart testing, eye testing, micro chip/tattoo, breathing and hearing.

The French Bulldog Club of America has no obligatory health checks either. The breeders, who are a member of their Breeding Club, have the intention to breed only in order to improve the health and temperament of the French Bulldog. On the website of the American Breeding Club a "Breeders Recommendation" can be found. In this recommendation it is advised to have the breeding stock checked for hereditary eye-diseases, X-raying them etc.

Both the UK Kennel Club and American Kennel Club run a puppy referral service on their websites, and help to place adult dogs that can no longer be kept by their owners due to personal circumstances.

Finally, you must also realise that a pedigree is nothing more or less than evidence of descent. A pedigree says nothing about the health of the parent dogs and the puppies.

Take your time when buying a French Bulldog puppy

Hopefully your Frenchie will live with you the next 13 to 14 years, so it is worth to take the time that is needed to buy a good puppy. The most reputable breeders do not advertise. They put all their effort in producing a good health, a good temperament, and a good conformation. Most of the time, these breeders have waiting lists for their puppies and this certainly is the way that it should be when breeding dogs. These breeders do not sell their puppies to every possible buyer, they only want to give their puppies the very best of new homes.

The price that has to be paid for a French Bulldog often is considered to be too high. However, you should bear in mind, that most of the time French Bulldog litters are small, the stud fee is high, reputable breeders make a lot of cost for health tests and very often the puppies are born via a caesarean section. This altogether makes it very expensive to breed French Bulldogs.

Things to watch out for

Buying a puppy is a huge responsibility, and there is a lot to consider. Here is a checklist to help you make the right choice:

- Never buy a puppy on an impulse, even if it is love at first sight. A dog is a living being that will need a lot of care and attention over its long life. It is not a toy that you can ignore or grow tired of. By buying a puppy you are taking on a huge responsibility, but you will be rewarded by a love and companionship over many happy years!
- Never buy your puppy through a pet shop, a puppy farm, the Internet or from one of the free newspapers that is the worst possible way to buy a puppy.
- Take a good look at the mother. Is she calm, nervous, aggressive, well cared-for or neglected? The behaviour and condition of the mother is not only a sign of the quality of the breeder, but also of the puppy you are about to buy.
- Avoid buying a puppy whose mother appears to have little contact with humans. A young dog needs as many stimuli and experiences as possible during its early months. Exposure to the breeder's family means it can get used to humans, other pets and different sights and sounds. Kennel dogs miss these experiences and have often not been sufficiently socialised.
- Always ask to see the papers of the parents (vaccination certificates, pedigrees, official reports on health examinations such as hip- and eye-checks).
- Check whether the pups have been vaccinated and wormed. It is important you have a written record of any treatment administered to your puppy that you will be able to show your vet.
- Never buy a puppy younger than eight weeks.
- Put any agreement with the breeder in writing. A model agreement is available from the Kennel Club or from the Breed Association.

Ten golden puppy rules

1. Walk your puppy for no more than 20 minutes, followed by a short play, and then some hours sleep.
2. Never let a puppy run endlessly after a ball.
3. Do not let your puppy romp with large, heavy dogs.
4. Do not let your puppy play on a full stomach.
5. Never feed your puppy immediately after exercise.
6. Do not let your puppy go up and down the stairs in its first year. Also be careful with smooth floors.
7. Never add supplements to complete dog food.
8. Watch you puppy's weight. Being overweight can lead to many health problems.
9. Give your puppy a quiet place to sleep.
10. Pick up your puppy carefully, one hand under its chest and the other hand under its hindquarters.

Shopping list

- Collar
- Lead
- ID tag
- Blanket
- Water bowl
- Food bowl
- Poop scoop
- Food
- Comb
- Brush
- Toys
- Dog basket
- Indoor kennel/crate

Travelling

Travelling with a dog is not always fun. Some dogs love a trip in the car, while others need a lot of coaxing even to get them in! Dogs can also suffer from carsickness, and if you are planning a holiday and want to take your dog with you, you should spend time getting them used to journeys.

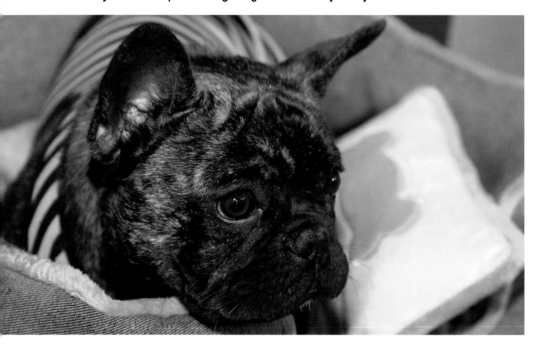

Travelling with your French Bulldog

The most serious and life threatening situation for a French Bulldog is to be left alone in a car when it is warm outside or to be separated from its owner in a stressful situation as the combination of stress and heat can be fatal.

NEVER, NEVER leave your French Bulldog unattended in a car, not even for a few minutes. Never travel long distances with your French Bulldog in the car, unless you make adequate provision in case of an emergency. Even if you have air conditioning in your car, you should not take your French Bulldog with you on long distances. Take plenty of cool water with you and make sure that it has suitable shade from the sun. There also has to be a free flow of air through the car. During very hot weather you can use semi frozen bottles of water (the square plastic bottles are ideal), when they thaw they will give you a supply of ice cold water. Placed in the box of your French Bulldog and covered with a towel, this will also help to keep your dog cool. If you put wet towels in the freezer and then store them in a cool box they make an excellent cool bed for your dog to lie on. The lightweight canvas cages are not recommended to use for your French Bulldog, as they do not allow an adequate airflow.

Before you plan to travel to a show, think about all this. Remember that there is no prize or championship at a dog show, which is ever worth the life of your French Bulldog. STRESS AND HEAT ARE A LETHAL COMBINATION.

That very first trip

The first trip of a puppy's life - from the breeder to its new home - is also the most nerve-wracking. If possible, pick up your puppy in the early morning, as this will give him the whole day to get used to his new environment. Ask the breeder not to feed your puppy on that day to avoid stomach upsets or carsickness en route home. Your puppy will be overwhelmed by all the new experiences and by leaving his mother and littermates. It has to go into a small space (the car) with all its new smells, noises and strange people. So there is a big chance that the puppy will be carsick this first time, with the possible consequence that it will remember travelling in the car as an unpleasant experience.

So it is important to make this first trip as pleasant as possible. When picking up a puppy, always take someone with you who can sit on the back seat with the puppy on his or her lap and talk to it calmly. It can happen that the puppy, in its nervousness, may urinate or be sick, so it is useful to take an old towel in the car.

Ask the breeder for a cloth or something else from the puppies' basket or bed that carries a familiar scent. The puppy can lie on this in the car, and this will also help if it feels lonely during the first nights at home. If the trip home is a long one, then stop for a break once in a while. Let your puppy roam and sniff around on the lead providing the area is free of other dogs. Offer it something to drink and, if necessary, let it go to the toilet. It is also good advice to give a puppy positive experiences with car journeys. Make short trips to places where you can walk and play with it. After all, once in a while you will have to take your dog to certain places, such as to the veterinarian or to visit friends or acquaintances.

Carsickness

Walking a dog on the beach or in the woods is a good way to escape from the stress of day-by-day life - and dogs love it too! Often the first stage is a trip in the car. Most dogs have absolutely no problem with travelling, but some suffer from carsickness.

Many puppies suffer from nausea and vomiting on their first journey to their new home. The combination of fear and the car's motion plays a major role here and most puppies are only sick on this one occasion. However, for some dogs travel sickness can be a life-long problem and they can suffer terribly. If your French Bulldog continues to suffer beyond its early puppyhood, consult a vet about possible medication for this. The best way to get a puppy used to the car is to make lots of very short trips at first, with the puppy safely secured in a travel crate. It is very important that the puppy goes for a walk first and has had nothing to eat for four or five hours. Ensure the journey ends with a good destination, such as the woods, so your puppy associates the car with positive experiences. If things go well, reward your puppy and then drive quietly home again. Never punish your dog if it whines or vomits during a car trip. The best thing is to pay no attention to it.

NEVER drag your dog into the car on its lead, instead coax it using positive reinforcement. If these short journeys go well, slowly build up the distance. It is also important to adjust your driving style where possible. Try and maintain a steady speed with no sudden braking, strong acceleration or sharp cornering.

Taking your French Bulldog on holiday

When making holiday plans you will need to consider what you will do with your French Bulldog. Are you taking it with you, putting it into a boarding kennel or leaving it with friends? What ever you decide will involve extra thought and planning in advance. If you choose to holiday with your dog, you need to be sure he will be welcome at your holiday home. If you are in the UK and going abroad it will need certain vaccinations and a health certificate, which normally needs to be done four weeks before departure. You must also be sure that you have made all the arrangements necessary to bring your dog back home without it needing to go into quarantine under the rabies regulations. Your vet can give you the most recent information. If your trip goes to southern Europe, ask for a treatment against ticks (you can read more about this in the chapter on parasites).

Although taking your dog on holiday can be part of the joy of ownership, you must seriously ask yourself if the dog is going to enjoy it as well. French Bulldogs really suffer in hot countries and long days spent travelling in a car is equally unpleasant for many dogs. If you do decide to take your dog with you, make regular stops at safe places during your journey, so that your dog can have a good run, take plenty of fresh drinking water with you, as well as a good supply of your dog's usual diet. Never leave your dog in the car when the sun is shining. The temperature can quickly climb, leaving the dog in an awful and life-threatening situation. If you cannot avoid it, park the car in the shade and leave a window open for a little fresh air. Even if you have taken these precautions, frequently check on your dog and never stay away longer than is strictly necessary.

If you are travelling by plane or ship, leave plenty of time to make the necessary arrangements for your dog before you travel and investigate fully the rules that need to be observed. If you decide not to take your dog with you, you must find a place for him to stay while you are away. There are special boarding kennels for French Bulldogs, but it is essential you book in advance, especially during busy summer holiday months. The kennel may also require certain vaccinations, which need to be given at least one month before the stay.

You may decide to employ a 'dog sitter' to come and stay in your own house and care for your dog. This also needs to be arranged well in advance and you must allocate time before you leave for the sitter to become acquainted with your dog and his routine. Always ensure that your dog can be traced in case it should run away or get lost while you are on holiday. A tag with home and holiday address and a mobile telephone number can prevent a lot of problems.

Moving home

Dogs are generally more attached to the humans they live with than to the house they live in. Moving home is usually not a problem for them, but it can be useful before moving to familiarise your dog with his new home and the surrounding area. It is a good idea to leave your dog with relatives or friends or in a boarding kennel on the day of the move, this will reduce the chances of your dog becoming confused and getting lost during the stress of the move. When your move is complete, you can pick your dog up and let him settle quietly into his new home. Make sure you set up his bed immediately so he has somewhere familiar to go to in the new home.

During the first week or so, always walk your dog on a lead, because an animal can also get lost in new surroundings, and take different routes so he quickly gets to know the neighbourhood. Do not forget to get your new address and phone number engraved on the dog's tag. Send a change of address notice to the institution that has the microchip data.

Keep Your French Bulldog Cool

A heat stroke can kill your French Bulldog. Heat stroke is an emergency, which can be life threatening. For that reason it is important that French Bulldog owners learn to recognise the signs of a heat stroke, because the dog will require immediate treatment. French Bulldogs do not tolerate high temperatures as well as we humans do. Most short faced breeds have these problems. Dogs cannot sweat, they only can depend on rapid breathing to keep cool. By exchanging warm air when they breathe out with cooler surrounding air as they breathe in, they manage to regulate their body temperature. It is obvious, that when the air temperature is close to body temperature, cooling by rapid breathing will not be very successful.

Signs of a heat stroke

A heat stroke is evident by the typical appearance of the dog, and it can be confirmed by taking its temperature. A heat stroke starts rapid, frantic, noisy breathing. The tongue and the inside of the mouth are bright red. The dogs saliva is thick and hangs in drools or it may appear frothy. The dog frequently vomits. The eyes have a frantic bulbous look.

Your French Bulldog really will be in serious trouble if these signs continue as within a very short time the dogs lips and tongue turn blue and the eyes may glaze over. The dog becomes unsteady and staggers. It may have diarrhoea and it will become progressively weaker. Coma and death can follow. All this happens within a few minutes.

Treatment

When you think that your dog is overheating, you have to take emergency measures immediately. When it is not too bad, you can move the dog to cooler surroundings and offer it frequently a small amount of water. In case the dog is showing more serious signs (as described above) or if you are not sure about it, you can cool down your French Bulldog by immersion in of his body in cool water, or by being hosed down with a garden hose. In emergency cases an ice cube gently inserted in the rectum also helps. A heat stroke can also be accompanied by swelling of the throat, the dog will 'roar' or 'rasp' when breathing, this aggravates the problem by reducing the airflow causing the dog to panic and get even more stressed. This situation requires veterinary treatment immediately, the vet will usually administer a cortisone injection to reduce swelling. He may also administer a cool water enema.

Prevention

Do not expose your French Bulldog to prolonged heat. Restrict exercise during the heat of the day. Provide your French Bulldog with shade and water if you are outside, even in the garden. See that your French Bulldog does not get overexcited or stressed during hot weather.

Feeding

A dog's diet actually consists of a lot more than just meat. In the wild it would eat its prey complete with skin and fur, including the bones, stomach and intestines with semi-digested vegetable material. In this way the dog would supplement its meat menu with the vitamins and minerals it needs. This is also the basis for feeding a domestic dog.

Basic principles of dog food
In general
Dogs have always been primarily carnivores (meat eaters). However, in the wild a minor part of their daily diet consisted of vegetable material or the vegetable-based content of their prey's stomach and intestines. In the past, dogs kept as pets used to be fed the remains of the family dinner.

Today, most dogs are fed a diet of dry or canned food, and over the last fifteen years, the diets of our domestic dogs and cats have changed hugely. There has been a marked advance in expertise and the foodstuffs have become increasingly sophisticated. To fully understand the effects of the foods available, it is important to have some understanding of the anatomy and physiology of dogs.

Anatomy and physiology of the dog's digestive tract
Ingested food first passes into the mouth, where it is crunched; dogs have no lateral movement in their jaws and therefore cannot chew, but during this crunching, the food is broken down into smaller pieces and moistened with saliva. The dog's saliva does not include digestive enzymes, so true digestion does not begin in the mouth. After swallowing, the food passes through the oesophagus to the stomach, where it is mixed and kneaded with gastric acid, i.e. one of the digestive juices.

The gastric acid breaks down the proteins present in the food and kills off a large number of potentially harmful micro-organisms, which are also present.

Once the food pulp has been kneaded through thoroughly and fulfils a number of chemical requirements, the closing muscle (pylorus) of the stomach relaxes and the food passes through into the duodenum. The duodenum is the first part of the small intestine, here important digestive juices such as gall and the pancreatic juices are added to the food pulp. The gall juices help with the digestion of fat and the pancreatic juices contain enzymes, which help with the digestion of carbohydrates, proteins and fat.
Enzymes are substances which are produced by the animal itself and which help with chemical transformation during digestion.
The small intestine can be divided into three parts; the jejunum, ileum and caecum (appendix). The wall of the small intestine contains cells which provide the digestive juices, this wall has plenty of folds to provide as large a surface area as possible, where bacteria, which help in the digestive processes, and enzymes find a place to attach to. The actual digestion occurs in the small intestine and the foodstuffs are cut down into tiny pieces, which can be absorbed.

After being absorbed by the cells in the intestines, the nutrients are passed on to the blood, which transports the nutrients to the liver. The liver functions as a sort of traffic agent, which decides what needs to happen to the different nutrients and then sends them to the right place.

The large intestine (colon) follows on from the small intestine. The most important function here is to absorb the water from the food pulp. The intestine ends in the closing muscle (anus) via the rectum.

Food
Food contains many nutrients, which can be divided into six important groups: proteins, fats, carbohydrates, minerals, vitamins and water. Life cannot exist without water, but water does not actually contain any extra nutrients - unless it is mineral water, which can be very rich in certain minerals.

Proteins
Proteins look like a pearl necklace, consisting of different amino acids (the pearls). The amount and type of amino acids determines the characteristics of the protein in question. The presence of nitrogen in all amino acids is important for the development of tissue.

Proteins fulfil many functions in the body; they are the most important components of tissue, hormones and enzymes. Furthermore, they are responsible for maintaining water levels in the body, removing toxins and maintaining a good defence system. Proteins are found in both vegetable (grains, legumes, yeast) and animal (meat, fish, poultry, eggs) form. An adult dog must have at least (20g protein/1000kcal food) 8% protein in the dry matter of its food (NRC 1985; NRC 2006) to maintain its health. In fact, if you want to ensure optimum health, maximum performance and good appearance, this percentage must be higher.

The story that protein is bad for dogs has long been disregarded as a myth.

This was based on research carried out on rats, but at the end of the 1970s, research showed that the kidney metabolism of dogs is by no means as sensitive as that of rats. Since 1993, we also know that proteins do not have a detrimental impact on growth.

On the contrary, proteins, together with the right exercise, contribute to healthy muscles, which in turn stabilise the skeleton. This is a very important consideration for such conditions as hip dysplasia, for example. Proteins are a vital part of a healthy dog's diet, and a shortage of proteins will lead to anaemia, low resistance to illness, loss of muscle tissue, etc. A shortage of proteins is caused not only by insufficient absorption, but also through increased breakdown of proteins, which may be caused by many forms of stress (mental or physical strain on the individual animal). An influence of protein on behaviour is not yet clear.

Fat
The most important function of fats is to provide energy. Fats also provide unsaturated fatty acids, which fulfil important functions in the nervous systems and the skin's metabolism. In general fats in the food are very easily digested by dogs; they can digest as much as 95 - 98%. Dogs, like humans, prefer food with a higher fat content, which is why it is often added to dog food to make it 'tastier'. Fat is also important as it stores some vitamins.

Carbohydrates
Carbohydrates (such as starch and sugar) always originate in vegetable material. You can differentiate between digestible carbohydrates (starch, simple sugars) and non-digestible carbohydrates (cellulose, pectin), which come from the cell membranes and fibres of plants. Carbohydrates improve the transport of the food pulp in the intestines by stimulating the membrane of the intestines, this in turn, stimulates the peristaltic movement of the intestines. A disadvantage of carbohydrates is that they increase the volume of the faeces, as they also hold a lot of water. Fibres are a good compromise as they perform a similar function throughout the major part of the intestines, and are then broken down at the last stage by bacteria in the large intestine. Fibres are broken down into substances, which partly function as a source of food for the cells of the large intestine, beet pulp, for example, contains these valuable fibres.

Minerals

Minerals, in terms of the amount consumed, only play a minor role in your dog's diet, but nonetheless they are absolutely vital. As minerals are only needed in such small amounts, mistakes are easily made. Minerals are divided into macro-minerals and micro-minerals or trace elements. Calcium (Ca) and phosphorus (P) are well-known macro-minerals, they play an important part in building up the skeleton and, depending on the physiological phase, must be provided in the diet in a fixed relation to each other.

Other important macro-elements include: magnesium (Mg) (skeleton, enzymes), sodium (Na), potassium (K) and chlorine (Cl). Some examples of micro-minerals include: iron (Fe) (blood, oxygen transport), copper (Cu) (creation of pigment, blood), zinc (Zn) (enzymes, skin), manganese (Mn) (enzymes), iodine (I) (thyroid hormone) and selenium (Se) (muscle tissue, anti-oxidant).

Vitamins

Vitamins can be of both vegetable and animal origins. Vitamins are divided into two groups - water-soluble and non-water-soluble. Vitamins are also required in only very small amounts, and dogs are able to produce a number of vitamins themselves. On the next page we will list a number of important vitamins and their functions.

Energy

All organic processes require energy for the body to function, produce tissue and to maintain body temperature for example. The energy required must be provided by food. In principal, dogs eat until their energy requirements have been met. However, due to causes such as boredom, the feeding regime and the tastiness of the food, there are many dogs that eat more than they need and become overweight. Due to this risk it is important to regularly check your dog's weight to ensure he is healthy.

A dog will store energy reserves as fat on the ribcage. On shorthaired dogs, you must be able to see the last two ribs, and on longhaired dogs you must be able to feel the ribs. Initially, feed your dog with the amount recommended on the food packaging and check your dog's condition once a week. You can adjust the amount you feed according to your dogs individual needs (what is right for one, may be too much for another based on their metabolic rate, and level of activity) Increase the amount of food if the ribs are becoming too pronounced, and decrease the amount if the ribs are disappearing under a layer of fat!

Many puppies, particularly of breeds prone to skeletal growth problems, should be a little bit on the thinner side while growing.

Industrial food

Industrial dog foods can be divided into three categories depending on their moisture content: moist, semi-moist and dry food. Moist foods contain 70 - 85% water; the high moisture content makes it very tasty for dogs, but it spoils more easily, the quality is

Some important functions of vitamins

	function	shortage	excess
vitamin A	fertility, skin and eyes	fertility problems, night blindness	abnormal bone metabolism vitamin K deficiency
vitamin D3	bone metabolism	abnormal bone metabolism	abnormal bone metabolism, kidney malfunction
vitamin E	with Se protection, muscle cells, anti-oxidant	fertility problems, muscle dystrophy	
vitamin K	blood clotting	haemorrhages	
vitamin C	collagen metabolism, resistance, mucous membranes	connective tissue damage, haemorrhages, liver necrosis	
B1 (thimaine)	carbohydrate metabolism, nervous system	anorexia, circulation problems, diarrhoea, atrophic reproductive organs	
B2 (riboflavine)	catalyst, energy production, protein metabolism	anorexia, growth delays, circulation problems	
PP (niacine)	catalyst, resistance, skin and mucous membranes	skin problems, anorexia, diarrhoea	
B3 (pantothene acid)	part of coenzyme A, Krebs-cycle	alopecia, anorexia, diarrhoea	
B6 (pyridoxine)	catalyst protein metabolism	skin problems, haematological problems	
biotine	catalyst fatty acid synthesis	coat and skin problems	
folic acid	catalyst AZ synthesis	haematological and skin problems	
B12 (cyanocobalamine)	catalyst cystine/ methiomine metabolism	anaemia, alopecia, growth problems	

more difficult to maintain than with dry food, and it is relatively expensive. Semi-moist food is dry enough that it does not have to be packed into cans, but there are no real advantages to this type of food. Dogs might initially prefer it to dry food, but it is still easily spoiled due to its higher moisture content.

Dry foods are the most economical and do not generally go off, which means that they keep for a comparatively long time. The specific manufacturing process makes it easier to ensure constant high quality levels. Technically speaking, mixers can also be termed as dry food, until they have had water added, at this point, they also spoil quite quickly. If you want to compare different types of food with each other, you will need to look at the dry matter (= product without water) contents and ingredients.

It is very difficult to judge the quality of dog food as the packaging does not provide all the information and may not contain any quality claims. It is therefore a matter of personal choice, and you might want to request some further

information from the manufacturer. Generally speaking, though, as with most things in life, you get what you pay for. That does not automatically mean that the most expensive food is the best food as you may be paying for advertising and such. The amount of faeces also gives an indication: the more faeces, the lower the food quality. This, however, does not apply to fibre-rich foods, such as diet foods, "light foods", senior foods and diabetic foods.

Food quality
There are a number of important points regarding the quality of dog food: the digestibility, the biological value (degree to which the nutrients can be absorbed into the tissue), the manufacturing process and the circumstances under which the food is kept until consumption. Different terminology is used to indicate quality levels, the current product range includes super premium, premium, products for the medium segment and products for the economical segment. The lower the quality, the lower the price per kilogram. Top quality can only be delivered by manufacturers who have the best raw materials available, who conduct thorough research and who have a technologically advanced manufacturing process.

The first threat to the quality is oxidization of the ingredients. Light, oxygen and warmth are threats to food quality. Anti-oxidants are therefore essential in maintaining the quality of the ingredients.

This coupled with hygienic handling of the food during preparation ensures a top quality product. Good-quality food is packaged in airtight packaging, which also keeps out the light, includes a best before date, batch code and manufacturing date.

Physiological phases

A good diet should take the physiological phase of the individual dog into account. After all, the physiological phase largely determines what a dog needs in his diet. A growing dog produces a lot more tissue and therefore needs more building blocks than an adult dog. All these growth processes require a lot of energy, which means that the energy need is also higher, depending on the size of the dog, it will grow for 7 to 18 or even 24 months. During the growing period the puppy's digestive system is not fully developed and so can only cope with small volumes of food, it is important that the food is both energy dense (which allows for a smaller feeding volume) and balanced in nutrients for the age and stage in development. Puppies from a number of (usually) larger breeds have an increased risk of bone-related growth problems and must be fed a specifically adapted diet. It is also important to keep these puppies slim when they are growing, to prevent added stress on the skeleton.

Reproduction and lactation are very physically demanding on the bitch. When you consider that she has to produce both offspring and milk, it is logical that she will need to increase her energy levels. From the 6th week of the pregnancy, you will need to adjust the amount you feed. Energy demands also increase if your dog is very active, if there is a lot of stress on muscle tissue, it will need energy to repair itself from time to time and there is also increasing 'wear' on the blood, which means that more nutrients are needed to produce plenty of blood cells. If you keep your dog in an outdoor kennel, it might also require more energy to stay warm and it might be more active due to being kept outdoors.

By examining the needs of dogs in different physiological phases, it is possible to develop a diet, which fulfils specific requirements according to the dog's circumstances. Obviously, this type of dog food requires scientific research and high-quality raw materials, which will be reflected in its price.

Besides the physiological state of the dog, the size also affects the diet. Research has shown that there are many differences between small and large dogs; both in terms of susceptibility to health problems and in anatomy and physiology. The manufacturers of the best dog foods take these differences into account.

To give just a few examples of the physiological differences between large and small dog breeds:

	Small dog	Difference*	Large dog
Growth period	8 months	3	24 months
Range of growth	20x birth weight	5	100x birth weight
Length canine tooth	4-5 mm	3	15-16 mm
Energy needs	132 Kcal/kg BW**	3	45 Kcal/kg BW**
Weight digestive tract	7% BW**	>2	2.8% BW**
Life expectancy	> 12 years	+/- 3	7 years

* Difference = factor ** BW = body weight

Different breeds, naturally, have their specific size requirements, and every breed also has its own characteristics, such as a special coat or even breed-specific health conditions. Breed-specific diets are therefore becoming increasingly popular. These foods are based on the special nutritional needs of the breed and some foods also contain substances, which help to prevent breed-specific health problems developing.

Over the last few years, increasing attention has been paid to the possible effect of dog food in addressing potential health risks. Certain substances are added to the food, for example to increase the burning of fat (L-carnitine), to prevent diarrhoea in puppies (zeolite), to support the cartilage (glucosamine and chondroitine sulphate), etc. The right food can make a significant contribution to the overall health of your dog.

Important guidelines

In general
Buy food only in an undamaged, sealed package and take advice from experts (vet, pet shop owner or breeder). Buying in bulk might be economical, but make sure that you have a sealed food bin to store it in. Put a week's supply in a bucket, and place the rest in a food bin in a dark, cool place. Always make sure that you use up or throw away the last bit and clean out the bin regularly!

Puppy food
Buy the most suitable food for your puppy, according to the advice of your vet or breeder. The basis for a healthy adult life is laid in the growth period and food plays an important role in this.

Adult dog
Choose the food which best suits your dog and adapt the amount you feed according to its condition. Ensure you reassess this regularly as varying factors such as age, metabolic rate and level of activity can play a role in the amount of food your dog requires.

Pregnant dog

The amount of food a bitch requires increases from the 6th week of pregnancy. In the past, bitches were often fed puppy food in the last stage of the pregnancy or during lactation. However, with today's range of puppy foods, they might not all be suitable, so get expert advice on how best to feed your pregnant bitch.

Older dog

The dietary requirements of an older dog can change quite a lot. Scientifically speaking, older dogs need more easily digestible food, which stimulates the intestines, a normal protein content with high biological value and some support for the heart, the skeleton and to help boost its immune system.

Puppies, pregnant bitch and mother

Amount of food during pregnancy and suckling period

To ensure that the weight increase is no more than 20% on large bitches and no more than 30% on small bitches, it is important to keep a close eye on the weight of your pregnant bitch.

The more the weight increases, the higher the risk of problems during the birth. During pregnancy and suckling, the bitch must be fed a correctly composed diet to ensure that her food reserves are not completely exhausted. If she is fed inadequately during this highly demanding time, the bitch will have far more trouble recovering.

During pregnancy

A bitch is pregnant for approximately 63 days. Her food needs start to increase at around the 5th or 6th week of pregnancy. About 25% of the foetus develops during the first 6 weeks of the pregnancy; the remaining 75% of the foetus develops from weeks 6 to 9.

During the last trimester, your bitch will have a particularly high need for:
Energy: + 50 to 70%
Proteins: + 170 to 180%
Minerals: ++ (calcium, phosphorus)
Vitamins: ++

During suckling

The suckling period lasts for 4 to 5 weeks, and the puppies gradually suckle less from the 4th week onwards. While suckling her offspring, the bitch will have a much greater need for energy, as she must also produce the food for her litter. As mother's milk is very rich in energy and proteins, it is important that the bitch is fed a diet which is high in energy and proteins, and which is very easily digestible. The actual amount of food required varies hugely, and primarily depends on the size of the litter. The food needs of a suckling bitch may be as follows:

Energy: + 325%
Proteins: + 725%
Minerals: ++++ (calcium, phosphorus)
Vitamins: ++++

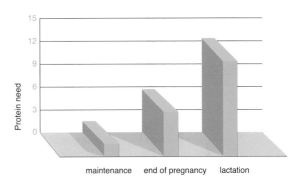

To prevent digestive problems, it is advisable to feed the bitch the same food from the last part of the pregnancy until the time that the puppies are fully weaned. The bitch's intestines are particularly sensitive to food changes during this important period. Within 24 hours, a puppy suckles more than twenty times from its mother. The bitch must produce 20 to 25% of a puppy's weight in milk to feed one puppy for one day (so multiply this by the number of puppies in the litter). The bitch may be fed ad lib during the suckling period, but do keep an eye on her condition.

Colostrum is the first milk that the bitch produces after the puppies are born. It is therefore very important that the puppies drink their mother's milk within the first 24 hours after birth. The colostrum contains anti-bodies against infections, which gives the puppies a good start to building up their own solid resistance. If the bitch produces too little milk, you will need to supplement it with special puppy milk.

Puppy during weaning

Immediately after birth the puppies depend entirely on their mother's milk as their only food source to stay alive. It is very important to check your puppies' growth during the first few days by weighing them at exactly the same time every day. Weaning must be a smooth and gradual transition, so that the puppy and its digestion gets used to a completely new diet. When the puppy changes from a liquid diet to a solid diet, it is advisable to do this via an extra step.

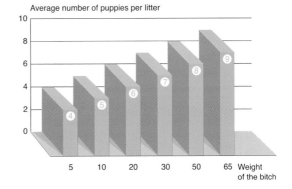

Energy: + 50 to 70%
Proteins: + 170 to 180%
Minerals: ++ (calcium, phosphorus)
Vitamins: ++

The increasing nutritional needs are best fulfilled by feeding the bitch a specifically composed diet from the fifth or sixth week on. Besides more energy, the bitch also needs more proteins and she needs a concentrated and easily digestible diet, as the uterus pushes onto the stomach during pregnancy, which decreases the stomach volume. The bitch therefore can no longer deal with large amounts of food.

Weaning - an important period

The first step in the weaning process begins after the third week, when you can start feeding the puppies small amounts of moistened food. During the weaning period, the puppies are quite prone to diarrhoea, which is at least partly due to their limited ability to digest starch. Compared to an adult dog, they only have a 5 -

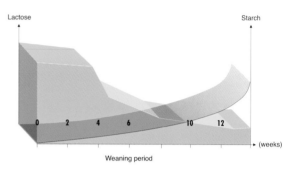

10% ability to digest starch (see picture). To minimise the risk of diarrhoea and to ensure optimum digestion, feed the puppy a food, which is easily digestible and has a low starch content.

Ready-made foods

It is not easy for the average pet owner to put together a complete menu for a dog, which includes all the necessary proteins, fats, vitamins and minerals in just the right proportions and quantities. Meat alone is certainly not a complete meal for a dog as it contains too little calcium. A calcium deficiency over time will lead to bone defects, and for a fast-growing puppy, this can lead to serious skeletal deformities.

If you mix the food yourself, you can easily give your dog too much in terms of vitamins and minerals, which can also be bad for his health. These problems can be easily avoided by feeding a ready-made food of a good brand. These products are well balanced and contain everything your dog needs, in this instance, supplements such as vitamin preparations are superfluous. The amount of food your dog needs depends on its weight and activity level and you can find guidelines for this on the food packaging. Split the food into two meals per day if possible and always ensure there is a bowl of fresh drinking water next to the food bowl.

It is vital that you give your dog the time to digest his food properly; do not let him outside straight after a meal. A dog should also never play on a full stomach as this can cause bloat (gastric torsion), where the stomach becomes overstretched due to an excessive gas content. This can be fatal to your dog.

Because the nutritional needs of a dog depend, among other things, on its age and way of life, there are many different types of dog food available. There are light foods for less active dogs, energy foods for working dogs and senior foods for the older dog.

Dry puppy foods
There is a wide assortment of puppy chunks on the market. These chunks contain a higher content of growth-promoting nutrients, such as protein and calcium. For small breeds such as the French Bulldog there are special puppy chunks for smaller breeds available. Other puppy chunks for larger dogs should not be given to a small breed like the French Bulldog. Give your puppy only special puppy chunks for smaller breeds.

Canned foods, mixer and dry foods
Ready-made foods available at pet shops or in the supermarket can roughly be split into canned food, mixer and dry food. Whichever form you choose ensure that it is a complete food with all the necessary ingredients. The information is usually on the packaging.

Most dogs love canned food, and although the better brands are of good quality and composition, they do have one disadvantage: they are soft. A dog fed only on canned food will not benefit from the gently abrasive effects of dry food on its teeth, and may potentially develop problems such as plaque, and/or periodontitis. Alongside canned food, give your dog hard foods or a chew especially designed for his oral care and hygiene.

Mixer is a food consisting of chunks, dried vegetables and grains where almost all moisture has been extracted. The advantages of feeding a mixer are that it is light and keeps well in storage and you need only add a certain amount of water and the meal is ready. It must never be fed without water, as without the extra fluid, the mixer will absorb the fluids present in the stomach, with serious results. Should your dog manage to get at the bag of mixer or dry chunks and devour its contents, give the dog very small amounts of water - half a cup - over extended (20 - 30 minutes) intervals.

Dry chunks have also had the moisture extracted but not to the same degree as the mixer. The advantage of dry foods is that they are hard, forcing the dog to crunch, removing plaque and massaging the gums.

Dog chew products

Once in a while you will want to treat your dog. However, avoid giving him bits of cheese or sausage as these contain too much salt and fat. There are various products available that a dog will find delicious and which are also healthy, especially for his teeth. You will find a large range of varying quality, and price in most pet shops. Always buy chew products that match the size of the dog.

Little shoes made from buffalo hide

The butcher's left-overs

The bones of slaughtered animals have traditionally been given to dogs and most dogs still consider them to be a great treat! But they are not without significant risks. Pork and poultry bones can splinter and cause serious injury to the intestines, so it is vital that you never give your dog this type of bone. However, beef bones are more suitable, as long as they have been cooked to kill off dangerous bacteria. Pet shops carry a range of smoked, cooked and dried abattoir left-over's, such as pigs' ears, tripe sticks and hoof chews.

Fresh meat

If you want to give your dog fresh meat occasionally always feed cooked (either boiled or roasted), never give it raw. Raw or partially cooked pork or chicken can contain life-threatening organisms. Chicken can be contaminated by the notorious salmonella bacteria, while pork can carry the incurable Aujeszky virus.

Buffalo or cowhide chews

Dog chews are mostly made of cowhide or buffalo hide. Chews are usually knotted or pressed hide and can come in the form of little shoes, twisted sticks, lollies, balls and various other shapes.

Munchy sticks

Munchy sticks are green, yellow, red or brown coloured sticks of various thicknesses.

Munchy sticks

They consist of ground buffalo hide with a number of often, undefined, additives. Dogs usually love them because these sticks have been dipped in the blood of slaughtered animals, but the composition and quality of these treats is not always clear. Always choose a product with clearly described ingredients.

Something to drink
A dog can go days without eating if it must, but definitely not without drinking! Make sure your French Bulldog always has a bowl of fresh water available. Food and water bowls of stainless steel are the easiest to keep clean and won't get chewed during the perils of puppyhood!

Overweight?
Today, obesity among dogs is an ever-increasing problem. A dog usually gains weight due to over-feeding and lack of exercise - medicines or disease are rarely the cause. Dogs that get too fat are often given too much food or too many treats between meals, and a dog often puts on weight following neutering or spaying. This is due to changes in hormone levels, making it less active, and less likely to burn energy. Finally, simply too little exercise and activity can lead to a dog becoming overweight.

To ascertain your dog is a healthy weight you should be able to feel its ribs, but not see them. If you cannot feel its ribs then your dog is too fat. Overweight dogs live a passive life; they play too little and tire quickly. They also suffer from all kinds of medical problems (problems with joints and the heart for example) as a consequence they usually die younger too.

So it is important to make sure your dog does not get too fat. Always follow the guidelines on food packaging, and adapt them if your dog is less active or gets lots of snacks. Try to make sure your dog gets plenty of exercise by playing and running with him as much as you can. If your dog starts to show signs of weight gain, you can switch to a low-calorie food. If he really is too fat and reducing his food quantity does not help, then a special diet is the only solution.

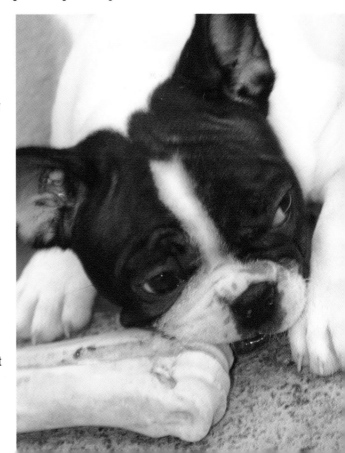

Care

Good daily care is extremely important for your dog. A well cared-for dog is less likely to become ill. Caring for your dog is not only necessary but also a pleasure. It is a wonderful chance for dog and owner to bond on a regular basis.

The coat

Caring for your French Bulldog's coat involves regular brushing and combing, as well as checking for parasites such as fleas. How often a dog needs to be brushed and combed depends on the length of its coat. French Bulldogs are less demanding in this respect, as a shorthaired dog needs very little maintenance outside the moulting season. A healthy French Bulldog has a shiny coat, which should be brushed once a week with a rubber massage brush. It is advisable to get a puppy used to being brushed from an early age by brushing it every day during its early puppyhood.

Brushing your dog every week should make bathing superfluous, and is not to be encouraged as the shampoo removes fat from the skin and coat. If, however, your dog has a good roll in something unpleasant, then wash it with a special dog shampoo, as the acidity level of your dog's skin is different to that of human skin, so it may well react to your own shampoo. A vet can prescribe special medicinal shampoos for some skin problems. Always follow the instructions to the letter.

During the moulting period (twice a year), you should give your French Bulldog's coat a stiff brushing every day. This is essential as brushing promotes the growth of the new coat and prevents your furniture being buried under dog hairs. Brush in both the direction the coat is growing and in the opposite direction until no more loose hairs come out of the coat.

It is important you use the right equipment for taking care of the coat. Combs should not be too sharp and you should use a rubber or natural hairbrush.

Good flea prevention is highly important to avoid skin and coat problems. Fleas must be treated not only on the dog itself but also in its surroundings *(see the chapter on Parasites)*. Coat problems can also occur due to an allergy to certain food substances, in such cases, a vet can prescribe a hypoallergenic diet.

Skin folds
The skin folds in the French Bulldog's face need to be checked at least once a week and need to be cleaned with a dry tissue. If the skin folds at the eyes are darker, it is due to excess tear gland discharge. You can smear Vaseline into the fold, so that the discharge doesn't get a chance to stick to the hairs. If the eye folds are very red, you can use zinc salve. The skin fold at the nose needs to be kept dry, too.

Eyes
A dog's eyes should be cleaned regularly as discharge can build up in the corners of the eye - you can easily remove it by wiping it downwards with your thumb or a piece of tissue or toilet paper.

Keeping your dog's eyes clean takes a matter of moments, but is an important daily task. Yellow discharge could be a sign of infection, in which case eye drops prescribed by the vet should quickly clear up the problem.

Ears
It is important that you check your French Bulldog's ears at least once a week. Their ear channels can sometimes be very narrow and can quickly become blocked and contaminated. If your dog's ears are very dirty or blocked with wax it is essential that you clean them. This should preferably be done with a clean cotton cloth (not cotton wool), moistened with lukewarm water or baby oil, or alternatively you can buy an ear cleaner from your vet. NEVER penetrate the ear canal with an object. If you neglect your dog's ears there is a significant risk of infection. A dog that is constantly scratching at its ears, or shaking its head may well be suffering from dirty ears, an ear infection or ear mites, in which case it is essential you contact your vet immediately.

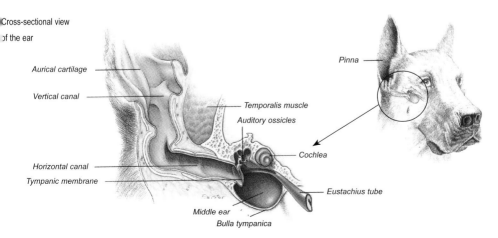

Cross-sectional view of the ear

Aurical cartilage
Vertical canal
Temporalis muscle
Auditory ossicles
Pinna
Cochlea
Horizontal canal
Tympanic membrane
Eustachius tube
Middle ear
Bulla tympanica

Nails

Nails usually wear down naturally if the dog regularly walks on hard surfaces, in which case there is no need to clip them. Nevertheless it is worth checking their length now and again, especially if your French Bulldog doesn't often walk on roads. Using a piece of paper, you can easily see whether its nails are too long - if you can push the paper between the nail and the ground when the dog is standing, then the nail is the right length.

Nails that are too long can become a problem as the dog can injure itself when scratching. You can buy special nail clippers in pet shops, but be careful not to clip back too far as you can cut into the quick, which can bleed profusely. If you feel unsure about carrying out this important task, ask a vet or a groom to do it for you.
Special attention is needed for the dewclaw, the nail on the inside of the hind leg, which needs clipping at regular intervals to ensure it does not cause an injury.

Tail

The small tail of the French Bulldog, sometimes shaped like a comma, can have a beautiful curl. However extra attention is needed when grooming your dog. The end of the tail sometimes tends to grow into the skin of the back. Of course this causes an infection and in that case, the skin around the tail has to be cleaned daily. You should do this with a salve that contains antibiotics. In the worst case, the end of the tail has to be removed surgically.

Teeth

French Bulldogs generally experience few dental problems, although they may suffer from tartar and bad breath in old age. To prevent this, you should have the teeth checked for tartar when taking your dog to the veterinarian for its annual vaccinations, as bad breath can be the result of dental problems. Bad breath can also be caused by stomach problems or certain foods. If this is the case it is advisable to switch to a different diet.

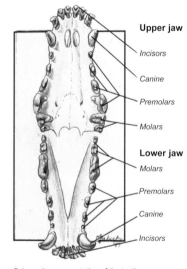

Schematic representation of the teeth

It is important that you check your dog's teeth regularly as it needs healthy teeth in order to eat properly and stay in good condition. If you suspect your dog is suffering from a dental problem consult your vet.
Regular feeds of hard dry food can also help keep your dog's teeth clean and healthy and there are special dog chews on the market that help prevent plaque and help keep your dog's breath fresh - but brushing your dog's teeth regularly is the best way of maintaining good dental health. You can use special toothbrushes for dogs, but a finger wrapped in a small piece of gauze will also do the job. Brush your dog's teeth throughout his puppyhood and he will soon grow used to it. You can even teach an older dog to have his teeth cleaned, use a dog chew as a reward and he will quickly learn to accept it.

Dental Plaque and strong breath

Dental care and a fresh breath are very normal for human beings. However this is not so natural for our dogs. Although the dog-owners get more and more aware of the fact that

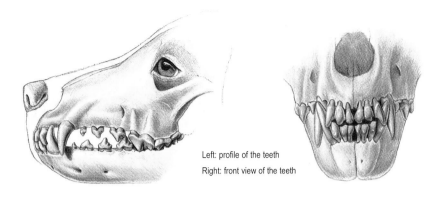

Left: profile of the teeth
Right: front view of the teeth

dental care is important for dogs as well, there still are many dogs that have a strong breath because of dental plaque or tartar.

In the first place, tartar is the cause of gingivitis, which spreads more and more and in the long run this even can cause problems to heart, kidneys and liver. So dental care is no redundant luxury!

The function of microbes

It is quite normal to have many microbes in the mouth. After every meal a thin layer of food stays behind on the teeth, which is a good culture medium for microbes. All this together is called dental plaque. The degradation products from microbes are acidic and they damage the teeth. As a result of this gingivitis and parodontitis are formed and as a consequence of that the dog might even loose its teeth. In addition to this it gets more and more difficult to clean the teeth when there is an irregular dental care. The fact is, that dental plaque will turn hard as the time goes by and then it is called tartar. Tartar can be removed by the veterinarian while the dog will be anaesthetized.

Parodontitis

Dogs fortunately have fewer problems with cavities. However parodontitis is the most frequent dental problem from dogs. When a dog has this dental problem the gums, the teeth and the dental alveolus will become affected by microbes in the mouth of the dog.

More than 80% of all adult pets, that are older than three years, find themselves in the different stages of this dental problem, and have suffered from a strong breath, pain and/or loss of teeth. In the long run, the microbes from the mouth can come into the blood and damage several important organs!

Additives in drinking water

Nowadays it is possible to add a tasty additive to the drinking water in order to prevent plaque, tartar and strong breath with dogs. This anti-plaque liquid can simply be added to the drinking water of the dog. This product contains the active substances chloro hexidine and xylitol, which restrain the increase of microbes in the mouth and because of that they prevent the building up of plaque. Apart from that, xylitol restrains the building up of tartar and takes care of a fresh breath. So every time that your dog drinks, the teeth are automatically taken care of. Refresh the drinking water every day, although there is some water left.

Regular check ups by the veterinarian

Apart from the daily dental care at home, it is to be advised to have a regular check up by the veterinarian. Gingivitis and other dental problems can be found in time. Dogs can hide their dental problems very well!

Your veterinarian will clean the teeth of your pet in a very professional way and he also has the right dental care products.

By following these simple procedures, you are helping your pet to a better and longer life. He will greatly appreciate it and he deserves it!

Anal glands

When a dog sits on his bum and tries to come forward by using only his forelegs (scooting), then you can be sure that its anal glands are bothering it. On the left and right side of the anus, the anal sacs of the dog can be found. In case these sacs are full they start itching and cause pain to the dogs. The dog tries to bite it and if you do not notice it immediately, your dog will bite it completely open. You can prevent this, by squeezing them out. However, if you do not know how to do this, please go to a veterinarian to solve this problem. You can also visit a professional dog-clipper.

Rearing

In order to enjoy dog ownership to the full it is important that you train your dog to be obedient. This does not have to be dull for you or your puppy, and if approached with the right attitude training can be fun and rewarding for both of you.
Praise and consistency are essential when training a dog. Rewarding your puppy for good behaviour with your voice, a pat or something tasty will soon teach it to be obedient. A puppy-training course can also be helpful.

When dealing with your dog, it is also useful to know something about the life and behaviour of dogs, and their ancestors (wolves, in the wild).

In the wild, wolves live in packs. Our domestic dogs view their human family as their pack. Every pack has a hierarchy, this means that there is one boss - the alpha animal - and all the other animals are ranked according to importance, right to the lowest position, the omega animal. There is a constant battle for the alpha spot in the pack. When you take a dog into your home, it is very important to make it clear where its place is in the family. This is simply done by following twelve rules. In this chapter, we deal with the 'rules of the pack', what they are, how you can apply them and what you can do and what you should not do.

The rules of the pack

Rule 1
The Alpha dog chooses a place to sleep, and no one challenges him.
The alpha dog chooses its own place to sleep and this is always respected by the animals lower in the hierarchy. If an animal lower in the hierarchy comes close to the resting alpha, the latter will growl to make it clear that the inferior dog must not approach. If the inferior animal approaches anyway, there is a real risk that the alpha will bite. This rule not only applies to resting and sleeping, it also includes access to places, which are prohibited to the inferior animal.
The alpha rules apply to any situation in which an animal high in the hierarchy asserts his authority over an inferior animal - it does not necessarily have to be the 'official' pack leader.

Advice
- Never let your dog sleep on your bed.
- The bedroom should ideally be forbidden territory for your dog.
- You can also prohibit access to other parts of the house. This makes it clear to the dog that you are higher in the hierarchy.
- Never try to take away your dog's safe place.
- Never let your dog take away your place.
- Never let your dog refuse people access to certain places.

Rule 2
The alpha male has the highest position.
In a pack of dogs, you often see the pack leader lying in a higher place than the rest of the pack, in order to assert his authority as the alpha dog.
Domestic dogs wishing to establish their dominance over you may attempt to lie in a high position – this behaviour must be stopped immediately to prevent your dog taking the alpha role in the pack. Dogs, which are lower down in the hierarchy, would never dare to demonstrate such behaviour.

Advice
- When you notice that your dog wants to lie on a higher position while you are present, do not allow it.
- If, for example you are sitting on the stairs and your dog comes to sit with you, make sure that it does not sit on a higher step than you.
- Never let your dog crawl on to your lap without your permission.

Rule 3
The alpha male eats first.
When the pack has caught a large prey, it is not necessarily divided up democratically. The alpha dog always eats first, possibly sharing with the alpha bitch. The rest of the pack must wait until the leader has finished.

The alpha male will decide when the rest of the pack gets its food. He may well decide that the others do not get anything at all, in which case he simply hides remains of the prey and moves away.

This can be seen as a challenge by the alpha to the inferior dogs. If an inferior animal dares to approach the food, the alpha will growl loudly and bite the challenger in the neck to correct it, or take the food away from it to display his higher position.

Advice
- Prepare your dog's food and place it out of reach, then go and have your dinner before feeding the dog.
  Only feed your dog when the whole family has finished. Place the food on the floor and give the 'stay' command before allowing your dog to approach his food.
- Place a toy on the floor close to your dog, and as he approaches remove the toy. Repeat this a few times and eventually the dog will soon stop trying to take the toy - this is the moment when your dog acknowledges your superiority.
- Never feed your dog anything while the family is having dinner as this gives the dog the same position in the hierarchy as you.
- Be careful with food envy! Never take food away from your dog and stay away from its food bowl when it is eating.

Food envy
Many dogs refuse to give up things they carry in their mouth (food, toys). If you do try to take these things from your dog, he is likely to growl. We can often see the same behaviour in dogs that are eating, this behaviour is called 'food envy' - and this is not acceptable behaviour. This can be prevented by training a puppy at young age that he should give up anything to his master that is asked of him. Training this with a toy that your puppy has to give up when asked, will prove to work well.

Rule 4
Playing, not fighting, is the way to establish hierarchy.
A dog can determine and confirm hierarchical positions during play. For young dogs, in particular, playing is also a way to learn to live in a group, and to slowly determine their status within the pack, as pet dogs often remain playful well into their old age.

If dogs constantly fought over their positions in the pack hierarchy, there would be a lot of casualties - in the wild an injured animal is extremely vulnerable and weakens the pack as a whole. Therefore dogs use play as a means of establishing the hierarchy. When two strange dogs meet they can respond to each other aggressively, as they are not members of the same pack, this has nothing to do with establishing a hierarchy, but with protecting their territory.

Territory
The territory is the domain of the pack. This territory may be several kilometres across and is divided into three different sectors. The outer circle of the territory is the first line of defence and pack members will make it clear to intruders that they are not welcome. If an intruder does manage to get through, into the middle circle, the pack will attack him. However, he will be given the chance to escape during this attack. The innermost circle is the centre of the pack, this is where puppies are reared and where the whole pack retreats to rest. Defending this area is a matter of life and death.
In the Western World humans live in very close proximity so it is not surprising that dogs have so many territorial conflicts. A dog will only view his garden as the centre of his territory, the rest is outside your garden fence. This means that the territories of dogs living close together overlap each other. Even when walking a dog on the lead a dog still has a territory. It is a mobile territory, and the dog sees itself as the centre, that needs to be defended.

It is therefore not surprising that two dogs often react aggressively to each other when taken out for a walk. After all, the centre of the territory must be defended.

Advice
- Always keep games under your control: make sure you determine the course of a game, not your dog.
- It is important to be aware that dogs use play as a means of establishing hierarchy - so make sure you always 'win' the game.
  If you think that your dog is trying to dominate the game, stop immediately and ignore him completely for a while.

Don'ts
- Never let your dog dominate the game
- Never let your dog determine how or what you are going to play - that is your decision.

Rule 5
The alpha wins every game.
When dogs are playing, you can see that a superior animal will always assume a higher position than an inferior animal. The superior animal will decide when the game is over and it will always win.

Advice
- Make sure that you always win the last game when playing with your dog. It is possible to let your dog win a game once in a while, but you must dominate the major part of it. How many games your dog is allowed to win depends on the hierarchical relationship between you and your dog. A dominant dog should never be allowed to win. A submissive dog can be allowed to feel like a winner once in a while.
- Never let your dog win the last game.
- Never finish a retrieve game by throwing the object, as if the dog ends up with the toy in his possession in his mind he will have 'won'. Equally, it is essential when playing a tug-of-war game that you finish the game in possession of the toy. It is particularly important in a tug-of-war game that you always start and end the game.

Rule 6
The alpha always has right of way.
If a superior animal moves through the pack, all the inferior animals will move out of its way.

Advice
- If your dog is coming towards you and wants to move past you, do not move aside - let him find a path around you.
- Always ensure your dog moves out of your path when required. Never step over a dog, even when it is asleep.

Rule 7
The highest in the hierarchy will always go through a narrow passageway first.
A narrow passageway is a very broad term in the domestic context. It is not only a doorway or a gate, but also the alleyway between two houses, the space between parked cars or even a forest path.

In a pack, when dogs are let out of their kennels, it is always the animal highest in the hierarchy that exits first. Dogs often run ahead when out on a walk.

Advice
- Open a door a little, If your dog wants to go through, close it - however, be very careful that your dog's nose does not get caught! Repeat this until your dog no longer attempts to go through the door, then exit first and allow your dog to follow.
- Sometimes your dog will try to go ahead of you through a passageway, which cannot be closed with a door or gate. In this case, keep your dog on a four to five metre long lead and walk towards the passageway. If your dog tries to go ahead, turn around and walk away from the entrance - the dog will feel a pull from the lead as it tightens and will quickly learn to follow you. Repeat these steps until your dog no longer attempts to go through the passageway first.

- You must never try to physically prevent a dog from going through a passageway first. If you try to discipline your dog in such a manner, it will soon learn that it simply has to be faster than you.
- Never let your dog pull on the lead.

Rule 8
All pack members pay respect to the alpha male every day.
All dogs in a pack confirm their submissive position every day by following the rules of the established hierarchy on a daily basis. They devote most of their time to the alpha dog, which they honour by greeting first for example. Everything that occurs within a pack reflects the hierarchy.

Advice
- Observe the rules of the pack on a daily basis.
- Always respect the hierarchy.
- Always show respect for those superior (for children, this is the parents).
- When eating, when wiping your feet after a walk or when going through a passageway, make sure that you always come first and that your dog always comes last.
- Always greet the highest members of the hierarchy first, this means that a dog must be greeted last according to its status within the pack.
- According to the rules of the pack, a superior animal must never let an inferior animal have an advantage - and this must be observed at all times. Never greet your dog before its superiors, as this will confuse its position within the hierarchy.

Rule 9
The alpha dog knows best.
The pack leader decides everything that goes on within a pack. He decides when to sleep, when to hunt, when to play, when to eat, etc. No other dog within the pack will make decisions that contradict those of the leader.

Advice
- As the boss, it is essential that you make all the decisions for your dog within the human/dog pack. You decide when your dog is allowed to go for a walk, to eat, play and sleep etc.
- Never let your dog decide. If he tries to persuade you to feed, play or take him for a walk, ignore him until you choose to initiate an activity.

Rule 10
An inferior member of the pack pays attention to the alpha.
The alpha never approaches an inferior animal, unless it wants to reprimand it.
An inferior animal always approaches a superior animal, and assumes a submissive posture (head low, ears back, tail low).

Active submission
Inferior dogs sometimes approach the alpha. In this case, they assume a low posture; the ears are pinned back, the tail is carried low and the body is generally held low and parallel to the ground. When an inferior animal reaches the superior, it will lick the corners of its mouth. This is a social gesture which dogs inherited from their ancestors, confirming its submissive position. We call this active submission - the inferior dog initiates the submission.

Passive submission
In passive submission, the inferior animal also assumes a low posture. However, in this instance the superior animal initiates the submission. The alpha approaches the inferior animal with a superior posture, and the inferior dog will react immediately and assume a submissive posture. If it does not do this, it will be reprimanded by the superior animal.

Advice
• Always make your dog approach you.
• Regularly play games of chase where your dog must follow you.
• Only ever approach your dog when you need to reprimand it.
• Never approach your dog, particularly when he is lying in his safe place.
  By initiating contact you are assuming an inferior position and are consequently undermining your position as the pack leader.

Rule 11
The alpha alone has the right to ignore other members of the pack.
The alpha will often ignore its inferiors as they pass by whereas the inferior would never dare to ignore its superior! In general, a pack leader will usually ignore the lowest members of the pack - and the job of caring for the youngest and most insignificant dogs usually falls to the rest of the group.
Every member of the pack must pay attention to the alpha. This ensures the group stays together - where the leader goes, the rest follow.

Advice

- Regularly ignore your dog when passing by, this confirms your position in the pack as his superior.
- It is advisable to ignore your dog if he starts to demand your attention too frequently. Try to avoid punishing your dog through negative reinforcement - to a dog any attention is better than no attention at all.
- Never let your dog ignore you, use plenty of positive reinforcement to maintain his interest in you.

Rule 12
A superior animal awards privileges to the rest of the pack.

Superior members of the pack will award privileges to those below it according to the inferior animals behaviour. Those at the bottom of the hierarchy are given the least privileges to maintain the pecking order. Equally, if an animal begins to misbehave its privileges can be withdrawn.

Advice

- Once you have established the hierarchy within your human/dog pack you can begin to award your dog some privileges by relaxing some of the pack rules. This will allow your dog to move a little closer to the rest of the family in terms of hierarchy, so it is important you still maintain some distance as the alpha member of the pack - the dog is not your equal!

Don't

- Never allow a dog privileges that are equal to other members of the pack as he will soon take advantage and attempt to challenge the established hierarchy.

Disobedience

French Bulldogs are intelligent dogs. Never listen to anyone telling you that French Bulldogs will never listen and are too stubborn to learn anything. As soon as your French Bulldog respects you, it will do anything for you, as long as it considered it carefully first. However, first you have to earn this respect by your own behaviour towards your French Bulldog. You cannot yell at your French Bulldog if you want it to obey, but you must encourage it with an enthusiastic voice. Make it feel that it is an honour for it to do something for you.

A disobedient dog is unpleasant for all concerned, and can make dog ownership a total misery! To avoid this it is vital you start your dog's training from the first day you bring him home. If you do not give your dog strict ground rules, and put an immediate stop to undesirable behaviour bad habits can quickly form. In the case of dog training, prevention is definitely better than cure! It is generally a good idea to attend an expert training class with your dog alongside regular training sessions at home. Always be consistent when training, reward good behaviour and correct annoying habits. Use positive, rather than negative reinforcement to establish a strong bond between you and your dog. This means ignoring anything negative and showering your dog with praise when he gets something right. For example, if your dog is slow to recall, do not punish him for making you wait when he eventually comes, as he will quickly associate you with negativity. Instead reward him for approaching you and he will quickly link you with positive experiences.

House-training

House training is one of the first, and most important lessons any puppy must learn. The basis for good house-training is total vigilance!

Always put a puppy out at the same times throughout the day; in the morning as soon as he is awake, before and after meals, every time he has been asleep or has been playing, and in the evenings before bedtime. Follow these rules and he will quickly learn where and when he is allowed to do his business. Praise him profusely each time he gets it right and allow him to play a little outside after he has relieved himself. If he does have the occasional accident in the house, take him outside immediately - do not punish him as he is learning, and the responsibility for this early training really lies with you.

Of course, it is not always possible to go out after every snack or snooze. Lay newspapers at different spots in the house. Whenever the pup needs to do its business, place it on a newspaper. After some time it will start to look for a place itself. Then start to reduce the number of newspapers until there is just one left, at the front or back door. The puppy will learn to go to the door if it needs to relieve itself. Then you put it on the lead and go out with it. Finally you can remove the last newspaper. Your puppy is now house-trained.

First exercises

To get the right result it is important to be clear and consistent during training. Commands should be short and clear, such as 'Lie down!' or 'Stay there!' Use a clear tone and ensure that each command is different so your puppy can distinguish each one It is important to be consistent once you have chosen the commands you are going to use, If you want the dog to lie down, it is no use using 'Lie down!' once and 'Lay!' the next time as this will prove to be very confusing.

Once the dog has understood the intention, it should only be necessary to call a command once, clearly and in an appropriate tone. If he does not react immediately, make a disapproving sound while walking towards him. Try to avoid shouting as this rarely has the desired effect. Dogs have exceptional hearing, and commands should be given in a quiet and preferably soft tone. Keep raising your voice for exceptional situations, and the shock factor will prove to be very effective!

The first lesson for any French Bulldog is to learn his name. Use it as much as possible from the first day onwards, followed by a friendly 'here'. Reward him with your voice and encourage him to come all the way up for a pat and a cuddle. Your puppy will quickly recognise the intention and has now learned its first command in a playful manner. Do not punish your young puppy as he is learning and will not be wilfully misbehaving. Once he has learnt this first important lesson you can move on gradually to basic commands such as 'Sit'. 'Down' and 'Stay'.

You can teach French Bulldog to sit by holding a tasty treat above his nose and slowly moving it back over his head. The puppy's head will also move backwards until its hind legs slowly go down, you can place an encouraging hand on his hindquarters too - at that moment say 'Sit! Once he is sitting reward him immediately with the treat. After a few attempts, he will quickly begin to make the connection between the command, the action, and the reward. Use the 'Sit!' command before you give your dog his food, put him on the lead or before he is allowed to cross the street.

You can teach your puppy the 'Down' command in a similar fashion. In this instance lure the dog down by moving the treat until your hand reaches the ground. The dog will also move its forepaws forwards and down, and you can help once again by placing your hand on his back and gently pressing. Use the command 'down' alongside this action and reward him as soon as his body reaches the floor.

You will need the help of another person to teach the command 'Come!'. One person holds the dog while the other stands at a distance of about fifteen metres before enthusiastically calling 'Come!' At this point the dog is released and should run towards the person calling him, where he should be showered with praise.

The stay command can be taught by first putting the dog into a 'Sit' or a 'Down' - then use the command 'Stay!' while showing him the palm of your hand before stepping back one pace. If the dog moves with you, quietly put it back in position, and repeat the command. Do not react angrily if he follows you as this is a learning curve and he will soon catch on. Once your French Bulldog stays reward him abundantly. Do not let leave him in a stay for more than a few seconds in the beginning. Once your puppy understands what is expected, you can gradually increase the time and distance of the stay.

Courses
It is strongly advisable to attend a training course with your French Bulldog to ensure he is given every chance to grow up in to your ideal dog. Fun and informative training courses are available across the country and are a great way for you to bond with your dog.
It is best to begin with a puppy course that is specially designed to provide the basic training and socialisation a dog needs to be a well-behaved citizen.

The class will also cover obedience and will help you teach your French Bulldog basic commands.

The next step after this is a course for young dogs. This course repeats the basic exercises learned during puppyhood and ensures that the growing dog does not get into bad habits. After this, the dog can move on to more complex obedience course for adult dogs. For more information on where to find suitable courses in your area, contact the Kennel Club.

Play and toys

There are lots of fun games you can play with your dog, such as retrieving, tug-of-war, hide-and-seek and catch. French Bulldogs adore all these games. A tennis ball is ideal for retrieving; and you can play tug-of-war with an old sock or a special tugging rope. Play tug-of-war only when your dog is at least one year old, as a puppy must first get its second teeth and then they need several months to strengthen.

You can use almost anything for a game of hide-and-seek, and a frisbee is ideal for catching games. Never use a very small ball when playing with your dog as it can easily get lodged in his throat.

Play is extremely important, as not only does it strengthen the bond between you and your dog but it also provides you both with plenty of exercise. Always make sure that you are in control of all play and start and end every game. Only finish the game when the dog has brought back the ball or frisbee, and make sure you always win the tug-of-war, as this will confirm your dominant position in the hierarchy. When you are not playing, keep the toys out of reach of the dog so he does not forget their significance. When choosing a special dog toy, remember that dogs can be quite destructive, even with toys they love - so always buy toys of good quality that cannot easily be destroyed.

Avoid playing with sticks and twigs with your dog as they can easily splinter, causing pieces of wood to stick in your dog's throat or intestines - potentially causing serious health problems. Equally, throwing sticks or twigs can be dangerous as they can get stuck in your dog's mouth, which again can be a serious health risk.

For people who want to do more, there are several other sporting alternatives that one can do with his French Bulldog. Behaviour, Obedience and Road Safety are some of the dog sports that can be done with a French Bulldog.

Aggression

French Bulldogs are rarely aggressive, however you may occasionally find your dog responds slightly aggressively to other animals or people. It's therefore a good idea to understand a little about the background of aggression in dogs.

In general there are two different types of aggressive behaviour; the anxious aggressive dog and the dominant aggressive dog.
An anxious aggressive dog will pull its ears back, show his teeth and adopt a position low to the ground. When a dog behaves in this way it is generally because he is very frightened and feels cornered. As he is unable to run away, an anxious aggressive dog will bite his victim anywhere he can in an attempt to defend himself as he feels under threat. The attack is usually brief and as soon as the dog can see a way to escape, he flees. In a confrontation with other dogs, the anxious aggressive dog will usually lose. However, if the people or dogs involved in the confrontation display fear he can become even more aggressive. If your dog starts to behave in this way it is essential you seek professional advice as the situation can easily escalate and become dangerous.

The dominant aggressive dog's body language is very different; his ears stand up and his tail is raised and stiff. The dominant aggressive dog is extremely self-assured and will hold a superior position within the hierarchy of his pack. The attack is a display of power rather than a consequence of fear. This dog needs to know who is the boss. It must be brought up rigorously and with a strong and consistent hand. An obedience course can help. Also you can seek professional help in dealing with this serious problem.

A dog may also bite when it is in pain as a natural defensive reaction. In this case try to reassure the dog as much as possible and reward him for letting you get to the painful spot. Be careful, because a dog in pain may also bite its owner. Muzzling can help in this situation. Never punish a dog for this type of aggression!

Fear

The source of anxious behaviour can often be traced to the first months of a dog's life - especially if there has been a lack of socialisation during this time. Puppyhood has a huge impact on behaviour in adult life and a dog that has never encountered humans, other dogs or animals during this period will be instinctively afraid of them later. This fear is common with French Bulldogs brought up in a barn or kennel, with almost no contact with humans. As mentioned above, fear can lead to aggressive behaviour, so it is important that a puppy gets as many new experiences as possible in the first months of his life. Take your puppy with you into town in the car or on the bus, walk with it down busy streets and allow it to have plenty of contact with humans, other dogs and other animals.

It is very difficult to turn an anxious, poorly socialised dog into a real pet - and you must be prepared to devote a huge amount of time and energy to the task. Ensure that you reward him often and give the dog plenty of time to adapt and, over time, he will learn to trust you and become less anxious. Try not to force an anxious dog into new experiences - instead use gentle coaxing techniques. An obedience class can also prove extremely helpful here. An anxious, unsocialised dog can be especially afraid of strangers.
Give visitors to your house a tasty treat to greet the dog with and he will soon start to associate new people with positive experiences.

Dogs are often frightened of things like thunderstorms and fireworks. In these cases try to ignore the anxious behaviour.
If you react to a dog's whimpering and whining, he will begin to see it as a means of attracting your attention, whereas if you ignore his fear completely, the dog will quickly learn that nothing is wrong. You can speed up this 'learning process' by rewarding positive behaviour.

Rewarding

Rewarding forms the foundations of good dog training. Rewarding good behaviour is far more effective than punishing bad behaviour - and is also a lot more fun! Over time dog training methods dogs have gradually changed. In the past the way to correct bad behaviour was often a sharp pull on the lead, whereas today, experts view rewarding as a positive means of reinforcing good behaviour. There are many ways to reward a dog; you can give him pat or a friendly word, or offer a tasty treat. Food is often the quickest way to teach a puppy, so make sure you always have something delicious in your pocket to reward good behaviour. Another form of reward is play. Reward a positive training session with a game with a special toy kept only for these occasions. As soon as you have finished playing, put the toy away, and your dog will soon start to associate it with good behaviour and positive experiences. Rewarding good behaviour is a fantastic training tool, but occasionally you may need to correct habitual bad behaviour. In this instance a firm 'no', followed by totally ignoring the dog should suffice. Again, consistency in all your actions is key in good upbringing of your French Bulldog.

Barking

Dogs that bark too much and too often are a nightmare for anyone within earshot! A dog-owner may tolerate barking up to a point, but neighbours are often annoyed by the unnecessary noise. Do not encourage your puppy to bark and yelp; and correct such behaviour with a firm 'quiet'.

A dog will sometimes bark for long periods when left alone as he may feel abandoned or afraid and is trying to get someone's attention. There are special training programmes for this problem, where dogs learn that being alone is nothing to be afraid of, and that their owner will always return.

You can gradually train your dog to become accustomed to being left alone. Leave the room and come back in at once, reward your dog if he stays quiet. Gradually increase

the length of your absences and keep rewarding as long as he remains calm and quiet. Never punish the dog after he has been barking as by then it is too late and he will not understand what he has done wrong - which could make the problem worse. Never go back into the room while the dog is barking, as he will view this as a reward. Leaving the radio switched on for company during your absence can sometimes help make the dog feel more relaxed. Eventually he will learn that you always return and will not feel the need to bark when left alone. If the problem does not seem to be resolving itself naturally consult a dog behaviourist or training expert.
Never leave your dog alone for more than a few hours.

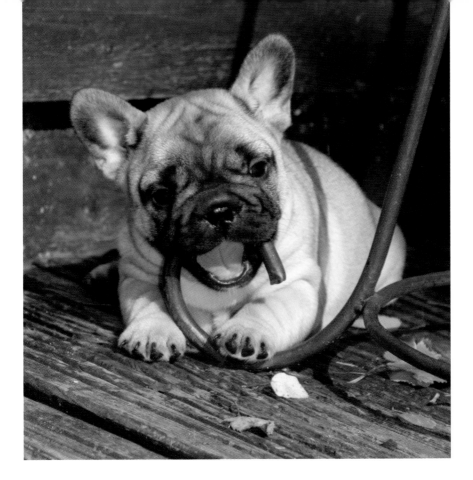

Destructiveness

Destructiveness is often the result of boredom. A bored dog will look for something to distract himself with, so always make sure your dog has enough toys and chews to keep him occupied. Do not give him too many toys at once, but instead provide a variety - which you can constantly swap around - keeping your dog entertained.

At four or five months your puppy will start teething. This often causes pain and irritation, which the dog will attempt to combat through chewing on things. Ensure that during this phase you provide your puppy with chews and try and keep him away from the furniture! Take care to take away the last small pieces of the chews, because a dog can quickly choke on it. A puppy will often take it in its mouth in one piece and it can then wind up stuck in its throat.

Chasing

Some dogs have the annoying habit of chasing other animals, joggers or cyclists. If your puppy starts to show an inclination to chase it is vital you immediately deal with this behaviour before it becomes a bad habit. The best way to do this is to do attention exercises with your dog.
Make sure that you are the most interesting and exciting thing in your puppy's world and try to keep his attention while tempting distractions pass you by. If your puppy stays focused on you - reward him lavishly!

Breeding

Dogs follow their instincts, and consequently breeding is a fairly straightforward process. Most pet owners choose not to breed from their dogs, but it is still worth knowing a little about it to help you understand why dogs behave the way they do.

Liability

If you are planning to breed from your French Bulldog it is important to be aware that a breeder is responsible for the quality of the puppies he breeds.

The Kennel Club places strict conditions on dogs used for breeding *(see the chapter "Health")*. If you want to breed a litter for fun, but do not have the relevant experience, you can ask the breed association for advice. Be extremely careful, because if the puppies you breed show any hereditary abnormalities in later life, you may be held liable by the new owners for any costs arising from inherited defects. The veterinary costs can be enormous, as well as the obvious implications of breeding dogs with significant health problems.

The female in season

It is a myth that it is better for a bitch's health to produce a litter. In reality, most spayed bitches lead long healthy lives, which are often improved by not having puppies! Bitches become sexually mature at about eight to twelve months, at which point they have their first season - which lasts for two or three weeks. During the first ten days they discharge little drops of blood and they become steadily more attractive to males. The bitch is fertile during the second half of her season, and will accept a male to mate. So the best time for mating is between the tenth and thirteenth day of her season. A bitch's first season is often shorter and lighter than those that follow.

If you do want to breed from your bitch, you must wait until after her first and the second season. Most bitches go into season twice per year.

If you do plan to breed with your French Bulldog in the future, then spaying is not an option to prevent unwanted offspring. A temporary solution is a contraceptive injection, although this is controversial because of possible side effects such as womb infections and the possibility of mamilla tumours when the female gets older.

Phantom pregnancy

A phantom pregnancy is actually not that uncommon. The female behaves as if she has a litter and takes all kinds of things to her basket and treats them like puppies. Her teats swell up and sometimes milk is actually produced. The female will sometimes behave aggressively towards humans or other animals, as if she is defending her young. Phantom pregnancies usually begin two months after a season and can last a number of weeks.

If it happens to a bitch once, it will often then occur after every season.
If this is a problem, spaying is the best solution, because continual phantom pregnancies increase the risk of womb or teat conditions. In the short term a hormone treatment is worth trying, also perhaps giving the animal homeopathic medicines. Camphor can help when teats are heavily swollen, but rubbing the teats with ice or a cold cloth (moisten and freeze) can also help relieve the pain. Feed the female less than usual, and make sure she gets enough attention and extra exercise.

Preparing to breed

If you do plan to breed a litter of puppies, you must first wait for your female to be physically and mentally ready. Be meticulous with your preparations and start searching for a suitable mate well in advance of the bitch's season. If your female is registered, and has passed all the health checks *(see the chapter Health)*, a breed club will you help to find a stud dog. If you plan to mate your bitch with a dog that has not been listed by the breeding club it is important you consider the following before you make your choice:

* Do not pick a dog without a pedigree.
* Ensure that the owner has the necessary paperwork confirming that he does not have any inherited defects.
* Observe the dog's character and temperament and look for characteristics that will reinforce the positive qualities of your bitch.
* Never breed from two animals of extremes together. If both parents are hyperactive, for example, there is a high chance that this undesirable trait will be even stronger in their offspring.
* Never breed from a French Bulldog with inherited or congenital defects.

The owner of the dog will generally ask for a cover fee for the mating, though occasionally, if they are particularly taken with the match they may ask for a puppy from the litter in lieu of payment.

Before mating your bitch, check that she is free of any parasites (external and internal). She must be fit, not overweight and vaccinated against all the usual diseases. If you want strong, healthy puppies, the mother-to-be must be in the best possible condition.

As soon as the female shows the first signs of being on heat, make an appointment with the owner of the male for the first mating attempt. In most cases, after the first attempt the bitch is brought to the dog again after two or three days to ensure the mating is a success.

It is important to be aware that accompanying a bitch through pregnancy, birth and the first eight to twelve weeks afterwards is a time-consuming affair. Don't expect to get much sleep, or time to yourself during your litter's first few weeks of life.

Pregnancy

It is often difficult to tell if a bitch is pregnant at first, and it usually only after about four weeks that you can feel the pups in her womb. At this point her she will start to put on weight, her teats will swell up and her behaviour will usually begin to change. The average pregnancy lasts 63 days, and costs the bitch more and more in terms of energy. In the initial stages of pregnancy she should be fed her normal amount of food, but her nutritional needs increase in jumps during the second half of the pregnancy. Give her approximately fifteen percent more food each week from the fifth week on, as she will need extra energy and proteins during this phase of her pregnancy. *(See the chapter on Feeding).*

During the last weeks you can give the bitch a concentrated food, rich in energy, such as dry puppy food. Divide this into several small portions per day, because she can no longer deal with large portions of food. Towards the end of the pregnancy, her energy needs can easily be one-and-a-half times more than usual.

After about seven weeks the mother will start to display signs of nesting, and will begin to look for a place to give birth to her pups.

This might be her own basket or a special birthing box. Ensure that the basket or box is in a quiet place and is ready at least one week before the birth, to give the mother time to get used to it.

Birth

An average litter of French Bulldog puppies counts about four puppies. Make sure that your vet knows when the birth is imminent, as French Bulldogs quite often have problems giving birth. Most French Bulldogs are born by caesarean section. The narrow hips of the female and the large heads of the puppies make that necessary.

The bitch will be very emotional after giving birth. Never leave her alone with her puppies during the first few weeks. In an attempt to protect her puppies, she might gather them together and smother them.

The caesarean section together with the anaesthesia risk, is one of the reasons that breeding French Bulldogs is not an easy task. By knowing this, one can understand, why people have to wait such a long time before they can have their French Bulldog puppy. And when knowing this, you also can understand why a French Bulldog puppy is rather expensive.

Suckling

After the birth, the mother starts to produce milk. The suckling period is very demanding as during the first three to four weeks the pups rely entirely on their mother's milk. During this time the bitch needs extra food and fluids - this can be up to three or four times the normal amount. If she is producing too little milk, you can supplement both the mother and her puppies with special puppy milk.

While the bitch is feeding the litter, divide the large quantity of food she needs into several small portions. Again, choose a concentrated, high-energy food and give her plenty of fresh drinking water - avoid cow's milk as this can upset the digestion and cause diarrhoea. Once the puppies are three weeks old you can start to supplement their diet with food. Start with specially designed starter food that complements the mother's milk, and can be easily digested. Start with one meal a day of starter food per week and gradually increase this.

When the puppies are seven weeks old, they should be fully weaned from their mother. At this point the bitch's milk production will slowly decrease, and her food intake should drop accordingly. Within a couple of weeks after weaning, the bitch's diet should have returned to normal (pre-pregnancy).

When you feed your puppies, make sure that each pup gets its fair share. If you feel that one pup is missing out, set it apart when feeding, but only do this as long as it is necessary. Try to get it eating with its brothers and sisters again as quickly as possible - as it is important each puppy learns to fend for itself in the pack.
Over-eating is just as dangerous as under-eating, so increase the amount gradually. Watch for the growth and behaviour of the pups and regularly check that their stools are properly formed. Small hard stools can be a sign of malnutrition or lack of fluids. Stools that are too soft or runny are often caused by overfeeding.

Neutering and spaying

If you are sure you don't want to breed from your bitch it is essential you have her spayed. During spaying, the uterus is surgically removed, after which the bitch no longer goes into season and cannot become pregnant. The best age for spaying is about eighteen months, when the bitch is more or less fully-grown.

A male dog can also be neutered if you do not wish to keep him as a stud dog. During neutering the testicles are removed, which is a simple procedure and usually uncomplicated.
There is no special age for neutering - where possible, wait until the dog is fully-grown.

Sports and shows

The temperament of the French Bulldog is vivacious, deeply affectionate and intelligent. It also has a strong desire to please and that makes it really nice to visit a course with your French Bulldog.

If you want to keep your young French Bulldog happy, you will have to do something together with it!

Many kennel clubs run their own sports activities and championships. If you regularly participate in activities with your French Bulldog, you will not only realise that the bond between master and dog has grown stronger, but also that your dog is quieter and more obedient at home.

Choosing a French Bulldog as a companion needs serious consideration, and means that you must be prepared to meet its physical and psychological needs.

Behaviour and obedience
You can pick from a whole range of obedience training courses, beginning with a puppy course. French Bulldogs usually enjoy this type of course. Their strong will to please means they want to perform the exercises as well as possible.
After elementary obedience courses, you can train your dog for various behaviour and obedience diplomas.

Obedience

You can follow up on basic obedience training by trying to pass the Behaviour and Obedience diplomas, classes 1, 2 & 3, with increasing degrees of difficulty. This discipline is also practised in a competitive environment, and there are British, European and World Championships. Among other things the dog must walk on the lead, follow at foot off the lead, stay standing or sit or lie for a set time while its master walks away and is out of sight for several minutes. Tracking and retrieving is trained and tested almost to perfection.

The British form of Obedience goes a step further; the accent here is on perfect performance of the set tasks. Highly intensive training is intended to make dog and master one unit, which, during the execution of several exercises, seems to be glued together. Obedience is only performed in competition, there are no diplomas.

As the French Bulldog is an independent thinker it does not often lend itself towards obedience competitions.

Road safety

Especially useful are road safety courses for dogs. Here, your French Bulldog can learn a few obedience exercises and at the end of the course can show you how safely it conducts itself in traffic.

Shows

If you plan to participate in dog shows with your French Bulldog, it is important to accept that to your dog this activity can be of little or no interest. Visiting a show is highly recommended if you want to learn more about a certain breed. You will also be able to get into direct contact with breeders and other owners.

Dog showing is a very competitive sport, in which breeders and exhibitors invest a lot of time. Some breeders even dedicate their lives to this. There are lots of things to consider before entering in your first show. Firstly, you need to choose which shows to enter and what you need to achieve for the dog to be awarded a title.

Showing a dog requires a lot of planning, you cannot simply start preparing your dog a few weeks before the show. If you are serious about the show ring you must begin show training your puppy from a very young age. In order to become Champion your dog needs to have three Challenge Certificates awarded by three different judges.
Of those three, at least one should be achieved when the dog is twelve months or older. Challenge Certificates can also be awarded to the best of each sex in a breed.

The British system allows a certain number of dogs per breed to be awarded the Challenge Certificate. The annual limit of Challenge Certificates to be awarded to representatives of a certain breed can be as many as 30 or as few as 6.
When the dogs enter the ring, the judge looks at them very carefully. Each dog is examined visually and physically by hand. The breed standards of most dog breeds contain remarks regarding the build - which the judge will be looking for in the show ring. The teeth will also be examined, as each breed standard will have its own notes regarding an undershot jaw or scissor bite. It is understandable that the judge will need to feel the dog in order to fully compare it to the breed standard. The breed standards also contain notes on gait and movement, which is why the judge will also need to see your dog move. Judges also pay attention to the carriage of the dog's head and tail.

Ring craft classes are a fantastic way to learn how to prepare yourself and your dog for the show ring.
The classes are usually very sociable events, where training is combined with lots of fun. Even if you do not plan to follow a showing career with your dog, it may still be a good idea to take it to a course. Your dog will learn to socialise with people that it does not know and with other dogs. It will also learn to walk on the lead properly without being distracted.

Some clubs that run ring craft classes also organise friendly unofficial shows and Companion Dog Shows for their members once in a while.

Types of Shows

There are many different types of shows. Here is a brief overview:

Single Breed Shows (for one breed only, organised by a breed club).
Companion Dog Shows (for charitable causes).
Open Shows.

Don't forget!

If you're planning to take your dog to a club or show you need to be well prepared. Don't forget the following:

For your dog:
- Food and water (and bowls)
- Dog blanket and bed
- Show lead
- Reward treats
- Grooming equipment
- A benching chain and collar

For yourself:
- Show documents
- Food and drink
- Clip for the catalogue number
- Chairs for an outdoor show

Parasites

All dogs are vulnerable to various sorts of parasites. Parasites are tiny creatures that live off another animal (the host), feeding on blood, skin and other body substances. There are two main types; internal parasites, which live within their host animal's body (tapeworm and roundworm for example) and external parasites which live on the animal's exterior, usually in its coat (fleas, lice and ticks), but also in its ears (ear mites).

Fleas

Fleas feed on a dog's blood. They not only cause itching and skin problems, but can also carry infections such as tapeworm and in large numbers they can cause anaemia. Dogs can also become allergic to a flea's saliva, which can cause serious skin conditions. It is important to treat your dog against fleas, and in order for treatment to be effective do not just treat the dog, but also his surroundings. For treatment of the animal, there are various medicines: drops for the neck, drops to put in food, flea collars, long-life sprays and flea powders. There are various sprays in pet shops that can be used to eradicate fleas in the dog's immediate surroundings (including the car). Choose a spray that kills both adult fleas and their larvae. Fleas can also affect other pets, which should also be treated at the same time. When spraying a room, cover any aquarium or fishbowl, as if the spray reaches the water, it can be fatal for your fish! Your vet and pet shop will have a wide range of flea treatments and can advise you on this subject.

Ticks

Ticks are small, spider-like parasites, which feed on the blood of the animal or person they have settled on. A tick looks like a tiny, grey-coloured leather bag with eight feet. When it has sucked itself full, it can easily increase to five to ten times its original size and becomes darker in colour. Dogs usually fall victim to ticks in bushes, woods or long grass.

Flea

Ticks not only irritate through blood sucking, but they can also carry a number of serious diseases. This is especially applicable in Mediterranean countries, where ticks can be infected with blood parasites. In the UK these diseases are fortunately less common, but Lyme disease, which can also affect humans, has reached our shores as well. Your vet can prescribe a special treatment if you are planning to take your dog to southern Europe. It is important to fight ticks as effectively as possible so check your dog regularly, especially when it has been running free in woods and bushes. Your dog can also wear an anti-tick collar.

Tick

Removing a tick is simple with a pair of tick tweezers. Grip the tick with the tweezers very close to the dog's skin, and carefully pull it out. You can also grip the tick between your fingers and by using a turning movement, pull it carefully out. You must disinfect the spot where the tick had been, using iodine to prevent infection. Never soak the tick in alcohol, ether or oil. In a shock reaction the tick may discharge the infected contents of its stomach into the dog's skin and infect your dog.

Puppy mange

Puppy mange, or "Demodex", affects almost all young dogs but does not cause problems for each one of them. The dog has little or no irritation, but some bald patches will appear on the head, neck and forepaws. A vet can often take biopsies of the skin to examine under the microscope and establish whether it is a case of puppy mange. Sometimes bacteria may play a major role and pussy blisters appear. Treatment consists of washing the dog with a substance that kills mites, of course this has to be done with the support of a vet.

Tapeworm

Worms

Dogs can suffer from various types of worm, the most common being tapeworm and roundworm. Tapeworm causes diarrhoea and a poor general condition. With a tapeworm infection you can sometimes find small pieces of the worm around the dog's anus or on its bed. In this case, the dog must be wormed immediately. You should also check your dog for fleas, which carry the tapeworm infection. Roundworm is a condition that reoccurs regularly and causes problems such as diarrhoea, loss of weight and stagnated growth, particularly in younger dogs - you may see evidence of the infestation in your dog's faeces. Puppies are commonly infected through their mother's milk. Your vet can prescribe medicines to prevent roundworm. In serious cases the pup becomes thin, but with a swollen belly, he may vomit up spaghetti like tendrils of the worms. A puppy must be treated against worms every two weeks from the third week after birth, until he is three months old. At this point the puppy can be treated every three months until he is a year old. Adult dogs should be treated every six months. If your dog is obviously infested you should treat him immediately.

Roundworm

Health

This section looks at the ailments and disorders that specifically affect the French Bulldog.

Breed-specific conditions

The most common and serious health problems with the French Bulldog are: Spinal Conditions (vertebral malformations, disc disease), Brachycephalic Syndrome (breathing problems because of its short face), Allergies and Orthopedic Conditions (hip dysplasia and patella luxatian).

Spinal Conditions
(Vertebral malformations and Disc Disease)

Apart from the breathing problems, the most important and serious built-in anatomical problem is the problem of the back.

These back problems are caused by the chondrodystrophic dwarfism that gives the French Bulldog its distinctive shape. Just like other dwarf breeds, they suffer from a high incidence of hemivertebrae and premature disc degeneration.

In the French Bulldog are found four types of vertebral anomalies;
  1. Hemivertebrae
  2. Block vertebrae
  3. Butterfly vertebrae
  4. Transitional vertebrae

The vertebral malformations are a collection of malformations of the spine from the dog. Most are not clinically significant, but they can cause compression of the spinal cord by deforming the vertebral canal or causing instability. All these conditions are congenital vertebral anomalies, which means that these malformations already are formed when the puppy still is in its mother's womb. Congenital vertebral anomalies include alterations of the shape and number of vertebrae.

1. Hemivertebrae

From the four mentioned spinal conditions, the hemivertebrae are the most likely to cause neurological problems. The hemivertebrae are wedge shaped, and therefore they can cause an angle in the spine. The most common location is the mid-thoracic vertebrae, particularly the 8th (T8).

Neurological signs result from severe angulation of the spine, narrowing of the spinal canal, instability of the spine, and luxation or fracture of the vertebrae. Signs include rear limb weakness or paralysis, urine or fecal incontinence, and spinal pain. Most cases of hemivertebrae have no or mild symptoms, so treatment is usually conservative. Severe cases may respond to surgical spinal cord decompression and vertebral stabilization. Hemivertebrae in dogs most of the time occurs in the tail, resulting in a screw-like shape of the tail. But it can also occur in the thoracic vertebrae. The French Bulldog is one of the affected dog breeds.

2. Block vertebrae

Block vertebrae occur when there is improper segmentation of the vertebrae, leading to parts of or to the entire vertebrae being fused. It can lead to an angle in the spine, but there are usually no symptoms. The sacrum is a normal block vertebrae.

3. Butterfly vertebrae

The butterfly vertebrae have a cleft through the body of the vertebrae and a funnel shape at the ends. On an X-ray, this gives the appearance of a butterfly. This malformation is caused by persistence of the notochord (which usually only remains as the center of the intervertebral disc) during vertebrae formation. There are usually no symptoms. Butterfly vertebrae occur in breeds such as Bulldogs, Pugs, Boston Terriers and French Bulldogs.

4. Transitional vertebrae

Transitional vertebrae have the characteristics of two types of vertebrae. The condition usually involves the vertebral arch or transverse processes. It occurs at the cervicothoracic, thoracolumbar, or lumbosacral junction. For instance, the transverse process of the last cervical vertebrae may resemble a rib. Transitional vertebrae at the lumbosacral junction can cause arthritis, disk changes, or spinal cord compression.

Allergies (skin and other)

Some French Bulldogs react allergic to various substances. We know contact-allergy, food-allergy, and allergy for substances that are taken in by breathing. Flea-allergy is also a well-known example. Allergy is shown through a reaction of the skin. These disorders can be temporarily, however they can also become chronic. The time of the year can play a major role with allergies.

The hair is often gone on similar spots, because the dog licks and bites it self, for these spots are itching. Get into touch with your veterinarian, because itching is worse than pain.

Brachycephalic Syndrome (palate, nares and breathing problems)

Brachycephalic syndrome is a group of conditions that cause resistance to the airflow through the upper respiratory tract (nose, larynx) in short-nosed breeds of dogs, just like the French Bulldog. This syndrome is caused by anatomic abnormalities related to the shortened bones of these dogs' compressed faces without the same proportionate shortening of the overlying soft tissues. The excess soft tissue leads to airway compromise.

Both males and females in a breed have the same problems.
Stenotic nares (pinched nostrils), overlong soft palate and everted laryngeal saccules are the most common conditions encountered in dogs with this problem. Although the abnormalities are present at birth, clinical signs of respiratory difficulty often begin in the early middle age.

Increased airway resistance from the brachycephalic syndrome over a long period of time can lead to progressive respiratory difficulty.

Especially French Bulldogs have a limited breathing capacity during stress and in hot weather, because few of them can breathe effectively with an open mouth and hanging tongue. For each French Bulldog owner it is important to know that his dog should NEVER GET OVERHEATED AND STRESSED OR OVER ACTIVATED IN HOT WEATHER! *For more information see the chapter "Travelling".*

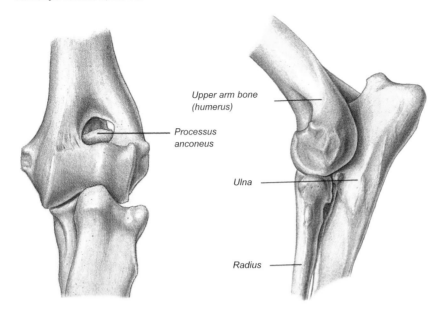

Upper arm bone
(humerus)

Processus
anconeus

Ulna

Radius

Orthopedic Conditions (hip dysplasia and patella luxatian)

Hip Dysplasia (HD)

The French Bulldog, as many other breeds, is vulnerable to HD. Hip Dysplasia is an abnormality of the hip joints in the hind quarters, whereby the socket of the hip joint and the head of the upper thigh do not match properly, This causes an inflammation and bone tumours, which can be very painful. Until recently, it was assumed that HD was primarily caused by genetic factors.

Recent investigations, however, indicate that while genetic factors certainly play a role in terms of a dog's susceptibility to HD, external factors such as food quality and exercise appear at least equally important. Limit the chance of HD as far as possible by giving your dog ready-made food of a good brand, and never add any supplements! Make sure your dog does not get too fat. A French Bulldog pup should be somewhat protected from HD in its first year. Do not let it romp too much with other dogs, chase sticks and balls too wildly or run up and down stairs. These kinds of games cause the pup to make abrupt and risky movements, which can overburden its soft joints. One important but under-estimated factor behind HD is the floor in your home. Parquet and tiled floors are much too slippery for a young dog. Regular slipping can cause complications that promote HD. If you have a smooth floor, it is advisable to lay blankets or old carpets in places the dog uses regularly. Let it spend lots of time in the garden, as grass is a perfect surface to run on.

The breed association tries to keep control by strictly testing potential breeding animals. An X-ray examination for HD is therefore recommended to all animals intended for breeding. The breeding stock needs to have a score sheet from the BVA, which the breeders should be happy to show you for both sire and dam.

Patella luxation

This is a problem in many small dog breeds, including the French Bulldog. Testing has proven it to be an inherited disorder in French Buldogs. In the case of this abnormality, the kneecap is not placed centrally at the end of the shinbone. The kneecap ends up next to the joint. A luxating kneecap can occur if the groove is not deep enough. This can be hereditary, but it can also be the result of trauma (an accident). In this case the luxation will be combined with ruptured ligaments. Patella luxation occurs in different severities. The amount of pain and discomfort varies per dog.

If the luxation is of minor gradation it can be sufficient to move the attachment of the knee ligaments. If the groove of the femur is not deep enough it must be deepened. Nowadays techniques are chosen to save the cartilage. The joint can be made tighter in order to keep the kneecap better on its place.

Slippery floors and strange movements (such as running after balls too wildly, bouncing and quick turns) are not healthy for the joints of any dogs, whether they are big or small, puppies or adults.

General anaesthesia

Please note that any time that a French Bulldog has to be anesthetized it should be done with a slowly administered injectable induction agent, intubation, and maintenance with the safest available inhalation agent. Never, ever "mask down" a French Bulldog or any other brachycephalic dog, as this is contraindicated in short-faced breeds.

Cleft palate

Though rarely, it may happen that a puppy is born with a smaller or larger opening in its palate. Such puppies show difficulties in sucking and - when doing so - one can notice small bubbles of milk coming out of the nostrils. In most severe cases, the affected puppies fade away and die within a few days. The condition seems to be hereditary but the mode of inheritance remains unknown. Checking the mouths of newborn puppies should be a part of the routine examination by the veterinarian.

Von Willebrand's disease

This is a bleeding disease characterized by excessive bleeding time due to delayed clotting. When there is a blood test available, which identifies carriers, affected and clear animals, though the test is sensitive to a number of criteria and hormone levels that affect scores. Research is close to develop a DNA test that will be much more effective in giving absolute information.

Diseases caused by viruses and other organisms

Pseudo rabies
Pseudo rabies or Aujeszky's disease is actually a disease found in pigs. The virus is trans-
ferred to other animals when they eat raw infected pork. The disease affects the central
nervous system, and a dog, which has been infected with the virus becomes restless,
apathetic, nervous and loses its appetite. Aujeszky's disease progresses incredibly quickly:
the animal will become paralysed and die within a week. There is no cure, so never feed
dogs (or other pets) raw or ill cooked pork.

Corona
Corona is a viral disease, the symptoms of which are vomiting and diarrhoea. This disease
looks like a parvo virus infection, but is less severe in its progress. Besides the symptoms
listed under parvo virus, other symptoms include damage to the mucous membranes,
which manifests itself in eye and nose discharge. The disease is spread via faeces.

Hepatitis
Hepatitis is a highly infectious liver disease. The virus is found in both dogs and foxes. The
noticeable symptoms vary widely. Approximately one week after infection, the body
temperature increases, after which the dog's temperature starts to fluctuate.
The dog remains lively during the first few days, but this quickly changes. Symptoms
include; coughing and an inflamed throat, moist eyes and a lack of appetite, sometimes
in combination with vomiting and/or diarrhoea.
The dog's eyes will cloud over and the virus is spread via the urine of infected dogs. As
infected dogs urinate in parks and against trees, the disease spreads very quickly.

Hepatitis symptoms vary from light fever to a very serious liver infection. If the disease is
treated at an early stage, there is a chance of full recovery, if the liver is infected,
however, the fever will run very high and the dog will no longer eat. Invariably, if the
disease reaches this stage the dog will die. Hepatitis can cause young dogs and puppies
to die very suddenly.

Hepatitis is not always easy to diagnose, as the symptoms are very similar to those of
Carré's disease.

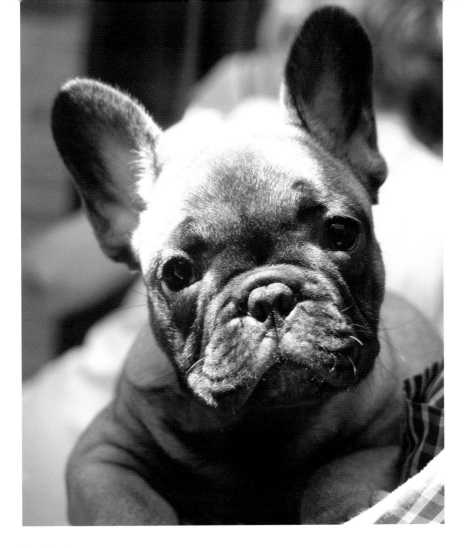

Carré's disease

This disease is caused by a virus and is highly infectious. The severity of the first symptoms, a runny nose and a cough, is often underestimated and shortly after this the dog will develop a fever, followed by a lack of appetite, vomiting and/or diarrhoea. Furthermore, the dog will suffer from an inflamed throat and discharge from the nose and eyes, spasms and cramps. A young dog may suddenly become severely ill. The virus causes inflammation in the intestines, but also leads to meningitis. Many dogs do not survive this disease, and the dogs that do survive, often suffer permanent nerve damage, or a 'tick'. Many dogs have behavioural disorders, which they did not have before the infection, e.g. orientation problems. The disease is spread via saliva, urine and faeces.

Rabies

This viral disease is fatal to humans and dogs. The virus enters the body when saliva from an infected animal reaches a wound of a hitherto healthy animal. It spreads via nerves to the brain, and will eventually kill the animal. Luckily, rabies does not exist in the UK, but if you are planning to take your dog abroad, you should have it vaccinated against rabies. Rabies is spread via the saliva (bites) of foxes, badgers and other animals.

Kennel cough

The kennel cough syndrome is caused by a number of different microorganisms: Para-influenza virus, Bordetella and others. The disease usually spreads when dogs are kept in close proximity to each other, such as in a kennel, dog hotel, at a show or at a training class. The symptoms of this respiratory problem are a harsh, rough cough and occasionally damage to the lungs.

Dogs do not usually become severely ill from kennel cough, but you must have your dog treated by a vet. Cough medicine (thyme syrup) can help to soften the mucous membranes and a holiday in a place with lots of fresh air can do wonders. If you are going to leave your dog in a boarding kennel, it is best (and usually also required) to have your dog vaccinated against kennel cough. You should have your dog vaccinated against this obnoxious cough approximately four weeks before it goes in to kennels. The disease is spread via the breath.

Parvo virus

Parvo virus is a highly infectious viral disease and an infected dog rarely survives. The virus is spread via the faeces of an infected dog, when a healthy dogs sniffs at these faeces, it immediately becomes infected. The virus penetrates the intestines, where it causes serious inflammation. Within a very short time, the dog will suffer bloody diarrhoea, may vomit blood, become drowsy, develop a fever and is suddenly very seriously ill.

The dog will usually refuse food or water and can therefore dehydrate. Treatment primarily consists of administering large amounts of fluid intravenously, however most dogs die within 48 hours of the first symptoms. In puppies, an infection with parvo virus can cause cardiac arrest, but today puppies are usually vaccinated against parvo virus very early in life. Puppies which have survived the disease may unfortunately die very suddenly later in life due to angina.

Weil's disease

Weil's disease (leptospirosis) is a disease caused by microorganisms. Dogs are most commonly infected in spring or autumn, and in younger dogs, the disease can often be fatal. A dog swimming in contaminated water might contract bacteria via the mucous membranes or tiny wounds on the skin, and from there, the bacteria gathers in the liver and kidneys. The symptoms include high fever, drowsiness and muscle pain.

Furthermore, the dog suffers from a lack of appetite, vomiting and is very thirsty. The dog may also suffer from nosebleeds, dark urine and sometimes yellow fever. The disease is spread via the urine of infected rats and dogs. Humans can also be infected through dogs or rats.

First aid for dogs

When your dog becomes injured or ill, the time that passes before professional veterinary help is available can be crucial. Whatever you do or do not do in this time can save your pet's life.

Remember that the first aid you apply is only intended to gain control over acute emergency situations. Your dog may have suffered internal injuries, which you are not aware of, therefore always take your dog to a veterinarian for examination!

If you are in any doubt about anything, ask your vet for advice. Applying medical aid to an animal always has one complication - communication with the patient - as you cannot explain to a dog that you are trying to help it and lessen its pain. A seriously injured animal is scared and in a lot of pain, and will therefore often try to escape or to attack its helper(s). It is essential that you gently restrain the dog so that you do not get hurt. At the same time, you must make it clear to the animal, through a firm but friendly approach, that you are sympathetic, but in control of the situation. Keep talking calmly and frequently address the animal by its name, the tone of your voice and the sound of his name will have a calming, relaxing effect. Persuade the dog to sit or lie on a table as this makes it more difficult for him to escape, and makes treatment easier for you.

Not all cases requiring first aid are the same, as one situation may be more severe than another and may require quicker intervention. There is a fixed order of treatment, from very severe to less severe. It is therefore very important to stick to this order when treating wounds and conditions.

In the overview on the next page you will see which life functions must be restored first, before you begin treating the next function.

Order of treatment
1. Respiration
2. Heart function
3. Blood vessels
4. Shock
5. Poisoning
6. Fractures
7. Digestive tract
8. Other injuries

1. Respiration

Together with the heart function, breathing is an animal's most important vital function. Breathing allows oxygen to be absorbed into the body, which is necessary to allow the organs and tissues to function properly. If the body becomes deficient in oxygen for too long, the organs and tissues will quickly become damaged and will eventually die off. If respiration stops, the animal is in acute danger. A dog with breathing difficulties often stretches its neck out and tries to inhale air with all its might; the mucous membranes of the tongue and the eyes turn blue and the animal will become unconscious after a while. If your dog is lying absolutely still and you cannot see anything on first sight, check the breathing by laying your hand or a few fingers on the chest: you should feel it moving up and down.

If your dog is struggling to breathe, take it in to the fresh air immediately. Try to discover what is the cause of the breathing difficulties as quickly as possible and eliminate it as soon as you can. Remove any possibly obstructing objects from the neck (collars, flea collars), and check that no objects are stuck in the throat or windpipe. In some cases you can apply a short thrust on the chest and push the object out with the air from the lungs. Applying pressure on the outside of the throat will also sometimes help.

If the dog is choking on water, you need to lift it up by its back legs with the head hanging down. This allows the fluid to drain from the lungs. Then push on the chest a few times to remove the last remaining fluid from the lungs.

If the dog is still experiencing breathing difficulties you will need to apply mouth-to-mouth resuscitation to your dog. Try to take the victim to the veterinarian as quickly as possible, continuing to apply mouth-to-mouth resuscitation during the journey.

Possible causes of respiratory problems:
• Too little oxygen in the environment (insufficient ventilation, plastic bag, box).
• Water, gas or smoke in the lungs (drowning, carbon monoxide, fire).
• Swallowed objects, swelling of the mucous membranes in the respiratory tract (asthmatic attack, inflammation), swelling of the tongue (wasp's sting).
• Restricted throat (collar, flea collar).
• Damage to the diaphragm, broken ribs.
• Damaged lungs.
• Suffocating on food (through fright) or vomit.

Loss of consciousness
A dog can lose consciousness for a number of reasons; epilepsy, a heavy blow, brain haemorrhaging and poisoning are just a few examples. If your dog loses consciousness you should always consider it an emergency, in which case you need to act as follows:
• Get someone to notify the vet straight away.
• Lay the dog on his side, as long as you cannot detect a wound there, with the paws pointing away from the body. The head needs to lie in a higher position than the rest of the body.
• Check the pulse. If necessary, apply heart massage.
• Check the respiration. If necessary, apply mouth-to-mouth resuscitation.
• When the dog is breathing again, pull its tongue out of its mouth and remove any food remains.
• Do not give the dog food or water.
• Keep the animal warm with a blanket.

2. Heart function

A dog can suffer from a heart attack, but not every heart attack results in a cardiac arrest. Some causes of heart attacks include drowning, suffocation, poisoning, severe allergic reaction, trauma or electric shock.

Symptoms include pain, shortness of breath, nausea or vomiting and dizziness.

Do not just assume that the symptoms will pass, if you suspect heart failure, you must take your dog to the veterinarian as quickly as possible.

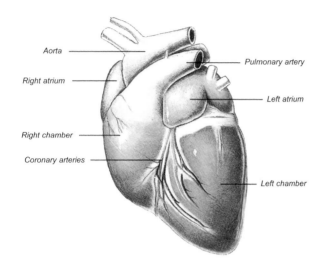

Aorta

Pulmonary artery

Right atrium

Left atrium

Right chamber

Coronary arteries

Left chamber

Above: schematic representation of the heart

Below: cross-sectional view of the heart

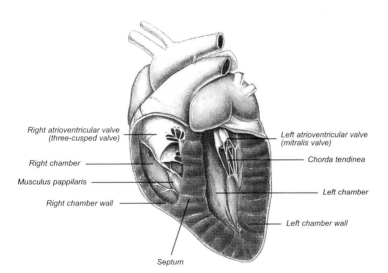

Right atrioventricular valve
(three-cusped valve)

Left atrioventricular valve
(mitralis valve)

Right chamber

Chorda tendinea

Musculus pappilaris

Right chamber wall

Left chamber

Left chamber wall

Septum

3. Blood vessels
Bleeding
A dog can become injured and lose blood. In the case of serious blood loss, the animal may die. How much blood is lost and how quickly depends on the size of the wound, but also on the type of blood vessel. We differentiate between three types of bleeding, depending on the type of blood vessel injured:

Capillary bleeding
This is a fairly harmless bleed; however, it does need to be treated. The wound is not deep (often only a scrape) and there is little loss of blood. Disinfect the wound well, and briefly press it closed with some gauze. You often do not even need to dress it.

Venous bleeding
In this type of bleeding the blood streams out of the wound steadily and is dark red in colour. This is because the blood is flowing towards the heart through the veins and is low in oxygen. Clean the wound well with a disinfectant tissue or sterile gauze soaked in boiled water and then dress it. Take your dog to the veterinarian straight away, they will again disinfect the wound thoroughly and stitch it if necessary.

Arterial bleeding

This is a very serious type of bleed, which can be fatal for your dog. The blood gushes out of the wound intermittently and is light red in colour. This is because it comes straight from the heart and contains a lot of oxygen. The dog loses a lot of blood in a very short time, and you therefore need to act very quickly.

• Hold the dog with a restraining grip and try to calm it. Use your voice to prevent it losing consciousness.
• First check respiration and pulse, and then try to stop the bleeding.
• Place the injured part at a higher angle than the rest of the body.
• Put sterile gauze or a clean cloth on the wound, and exert pressure with the palm of your hand, so that the blood vessel is squeezed tight. If necessary, put some extra gauze or cotton wool on the wound and exert more pressure. On spots where the skin is loose (lips, cheeks, scruff), tightly push the wound edges together in your fist.
• Once the bleeding has stopped, put a thick layer of cotton wool on the gauze or cloth. Bandage the wound with a tight bandage. Keep on exerting pressure.
• Take the dog to the veterinarian as quickly as possible.

Major bleeding at the foot or tail can be stopped by exerting pressure on one of the so-called pressure points with your finger. These are points where the blood vessels run closely under the skin and are easily squeezed tight.

If you cannot manage to stop arterial bleeding in the manner described above, you can apply a tourniquet as a last resort. A tourniquet must never be applied around the neck or head. After applying a tourniquet, take the dog to the veterinarian as quickly as possible. Be aware that a dog can go into shock as a result of serious bleeding.

Minor cut and stab wounds:

- Hold the dog in a restraining grip. It will probably try to resist.
- Wash your hands thoroughly and where possible use sterile material from a first aid kit.
- Remove any hairs that might be in the wound: dampen them with clean water, stroke them out of the wound and cut them off close to the skin. Examine the depth of the wound.
- Rinse the wound clean with a mild disinfectant, which is dissolved in water. You can also dissolve two teaspoons of salt in a litre of tap water. Try to gently rub open small deep stab wounds.
- Wash the skin around the wound with diluted disinfectant. Cover the wound with sterile gauze, to prevent suds getting in, and rinse with plenty of clean water afterwards.

- In graze wounds, in particular, there may be a lot of dirt in the skin. Remove it with a cotton bud or a corner of a clean cloth - but be very careful when doing this!
- Dab the wound dry with a clean, non-fluffy cloth.
- Put disinfectant salve on the wound and bandage it.
- Change the dressing every day and pay close attention to possible wound infections.
- If a scab has formed, you need to prevent the dog removing it. Keep the wound edges supple with Vaseline or cod-liver oil salve.

Major cuts or skin parts missing:

- In these cases your first aid attempts must be directed towards getting the animal to the veterinarian as quickly as possible, and to prevent the situation from worsening.
- The dog might be in a lot of pain, if necessary, apply a restraining grip.
- Remove any large objects, such as splinters, stones and twigs, from the wound. Do not remove objects that have deeply penetrated the skin. If they stick out of the wound, cut them off above the skin.
- Soak a clean cloth in a solution of two teaspoons of salt in one litre of water. Lay the wet cloth on the wound and secure it with tape or bandage clamps.
- Keep the cloth wet with the saline solution during the transport to the veterinarian.
- Make sure that the animal cannot lick or bite the wound.
- A deep wound needs to be stitched by a vet as soon as possible. This will speed up the healing process.

A dog can also suffer wounds when the skin is still intact. Examples of this are bruises or haemorrhages. You can treat these by applying ice cubes wrapped in a tea towel. Your dog can also suffer more serious, internal damage. Symptoms include lightening of the mucous membranes and/or bloody discharge or slime from the nose. In the case of internal injuries, you must not move your dog or allow it to drink - call a vet straight away!

Burns

The skin is a very important organ for any animal. It protects the body against damaging external influences by giving it the right signals (e.g. it is warm). The skin also sends signals from the animal to its surroundings, e.g. hairs standing up. The coat is covered with aromatic substances, sweat and fats, which come from the skin. Finally the skin also regulates the body's temperature and the dog's water balance; it makes sure that the body does not dehydrate in a warm environment. Burns can have serious consequences, especially when major parts of the skin have been affected. In these cases the skin can no longer fulfil its vital functions.

In the case of burns you always need to apply first aid. The animal will be in a lot of pain and will need to be examined by a vet as soon as possible. He will judge if the dog can be saved. Whether a dog can recover depends on the percentage of skin damaged and on how deeply the burn has penetrated the skin.

You can try to prevent the condition worsening by thoroughly cooling off the animal as quickly as possible. Proceed as follows:
• Cool the burnt part of the skin with cold water as soon as possible (if necessary by dumping the dog in a pond or bucket). The cold not only alleviates the pain, but also cools the skin, which prevents deeper skin layers being seriously damaged.
• You need to cool off the dog for at least ten minutes. Carefully dab dry the area around the affected spot, but do not touch the wound: the risk of infection is too great.
• Do not put any salve or grease on the wound.
• Cover the wound with a clean cloth soaked in a solution of two teaspoons of salt in a litre of water. Keep the cloth damp with this solution during your drive to the veterinarian.
• Give the dog small amounts of water - if it can still swallow - over short intervals (the mucous membranes of the throat and mouth may have been affected by the smoke).
• Burnt skin can no longer contain body warmth, which means that the dog may shake because of the cold. Keep it warm with a blanket.
• Even if your dog is obviously in a lot of pain, never give it painkillers or sedatives of your own accord.

Bite wounds

Occasionally, dogs can get bitten by a feral animal, such as a fox or a stray cat or dog. First of all, you should clean the wound with disinfectant, then take your dog to the veterinarian as quickly as possible for further treatment.

4. Shock

Shock is not actually a condition as such, but can be the result of serious injuries combined with severe blood loss, a bad fright or pain. An injured animal may also become stressed by your attempts to treat it, which can also easily lead to shock.

Preventing shock is actually more important than treating it, as a shocked animal has too little blood pumped through the body. If this continues for long, tissues and organs do not receive enough oxygen, so they start to die. If the brain gets insufficient oxygen, the animal will lose consciousness.

In cases where there is a real chance of the dog going into shock, you need to act as follows. Free the respiratory tract by pulling the tongue a little out of the mouth - checking first for any objects in the throat or mouth. If necessary, apply mouth-to-mouth resuscitation and/ or heart massage and stop any bleeding. An animal with very high fever or heatstroke (sunstroke) needs to be cooled with cold, wet cloths applied to the head and neck. Bring the dog into quiet, dark surroundings and make sure that the head is positioned a little higher than the rest of the body. If the dog has gone into shock keep him warm with a blanket and maybe with a hot water bottle (maximum 45°C). Alternatively, in the case of sunstroke, keep the dog cool.

If the animal can still drink, give it small amounts of water. Never offer it anything to drink if there is any suspicion of internal damage. Take your dog to the veterinarian as quickly as possible, they will put him on a drip to stabilise the blood pressure.

Causes of shock:
- Cardiac arrest
- Severe bleeding
- Dehydration
- Bad fright
- Severe pain
- Poisoning
- Allergies
- Brain trauma
- Serious burns
- Severe stress
- Malignant tumours
- Septicaemia
- Heatstroke
- High fever
- Prolonged vomiting/ diarrhea

Speedy actions can prevent your dog actually going into shock! If you see the following symptoms, you need to apply first aid immediately:
- Weak, irregular pulse
- Hectic, superficial breathing
- Cold ears and feet
- Pale skin (abdomen and inner thighs) and pale mucous membranes (mouth, eyes) and ears
- Apathy and anxiety

Epileptic seizure

A seizure can be of varying length. The dog will fall over and stay lying in an abnormal position with convulsions. It may urinate, drool or have widened pupils.

After a seizure your dog will be exhausted and gasping from the exertion and will be dull and uncoordinated. An epileptic fit looks very serious and can cause panic in anyone witnessing it, but with properly applied first aid, the whole situation is a lot less dramatic than it first looks. Therefore stay calm and proceed as follows:

- Carefully drag the dog by its back legs or body to a place where it cannot injure itself through its thrashing movements. For example, never leave it lying at the top of the stairs.
- Try to lessen the convulsions by putting a blanket or cloth over the animal and by surrounding it with cushions. This also decreases the risk of the animal injuring itself.
- Never try to apply a halter or hold the animal in a restraining grip and do not give your dog any food, water or medication.
- If necessary, apply mouth-to-mouth resuscitation, but watch your fingers when the dog starts breathing again.
- Allow the dog to come round in a calm, dark environment and stay and observe him for at least half an hour.
- If the seizures return within a short interval, you are facing an emergency situation. Take the animal to the veterinarian as soon as possible.

Heatstroke

A dog may be affected by heat, and this most often happens when the animal is left in a badly ventilated car. It cannot be stressed too often that a dog should never be left alone in a car in warm or sunny weather, even for a few minutes. Heatstroke can be recognised by the following symptoms: fast, jerky breathing, a glazed look and a body temperature of more than 40°C.

Take the dog to a shady, cool place and immerse it in a bucket or tub of cold water or hose it down. Cool off sparsely haired parts of the body, such as the belly, the elbows and the groin first. When the body temperature drops below 39°C you can start to dry the dog off and allow him small drinks of water at intervals of a few minutes. Take the dog to the veterinarian as soon as possible.

5. Poisoning

If an animal has been poisoned, it may develop a number of different symptoms. A poisoned dog will often have difficulty breathing, and will feel cold to touch as well as possibly losing consciousness. However, the dog may also start to shake and become hyperactive. Always remember that there is an increased chance of the dog going into shock.

Remove any remnants of the poison from its mouth or the skin with a cloth as quickly as possible. Try to find out what the poison is, and if possible take the package or whatever is left of the toxin to the veterinarian. This may be vital when it comes to determining the right antidote. How your dog is treated by the vet depends on the type of poison it has ingested.

If your dog has ingested something from the group of 'non-caustic' substances (see table), you need to make it vomit as quickly as possible. You can stimulate vomiting by placing a teaspoon of salt on the back of its tongue. Take a sample of the vomit to the veterinarian. If the dog is unconscious, lay its head lower than the rest of the body as this allows the vomit to flow out of its mouth and prevents it from flowing into the lungs. If necessary, apply mouth-to-mouth resuscitation. If the animal cannot be taken to a vet immediately, it is best to wrap it in a blanket and to take it to a dark, quiet place. Sometimes packages of toxins contain information on which substances need to be administered as antidotes. If the dog has thrown up properly, you can give it a mix of milk and Norit. This is advisable if it will take some time before you can take your dog to the veterinarian.

Non-caustic substances:	Caustic substances:
• Anti-freeze	• Base
• Bleach (chlorine)	- Caustic soda
• Carbamates	- Many paint or wallpaper strippers
• Pesticides:	• Petrol
- Strychnine	• Paint thinner
- Crimidine	• Acids
• Lead (paint and roof covering)	- Battery acid
• Insecticides:	- Hydrochloric acid
- Parathion	
- Dichlorvos	
• Snail poison	

If your pet has ingested a 'caustic' substance (see table), it must not throw up under any circumstances! The mucous membranes of the mouth, throat and gullet may have already been seriously damaged by the caustic toxin. If the toxin passes through them again, the damage will be more serious. Try to dilute the toxins in the digestive tract. In the case of a base toxin, give your dog vinegar or lemon juice. If your dog has ingested an acid, feed it soda or milk.

6. Fractures

Unfortunately, dogs quite regularly break or fracture bones. The prominent cause of fractures is road traffic accidents, but a fall from height, a bite by another animal or a gunshot wound may also lead to fractures. When applying first aid to fractures you need to be very careful, as the hard, sharp edges of the broken bone can easily damage tissues and organs.

Fractures can be differentiated into two groups. In closed fractures the skin has not been damaged and the fractured parts are therefore not exposed to the air. In open fractures the fractured parts break out of the skin through the wound. This type of fracture can have serious consequences, as the very sensitive bone marrow can become infected by bacteria. Such an infection can make an animal seriously ill and will slow down the healing process of the fracture.

An open fracture is obviously easy to diagnose. In the case of a closed fracture this is a little more difficult. There are, however, some symptoms which indicate a fracture: pain, swelling, loss of function in the broken limb, abnormal position of the bone, abnormal mobility of the broken limb and a grating sound during movement. When you have clearly diagnosed a fracture, you should proceed as follows:
- Hold your dog in a restraining grip and let it calm down as much as possible at the scene of the accident.
- Be aware of shock symptoms. They may occur if your dog is in a lot of pain.
- Make sure that the broken leg lies on top.
- Do not pull on the leg and make sure that the fracture is as still as possible.
- If the lower part of the leg is broken and if you need to transport the animal quite a distance, apply a preliminary splint. This can be a straight piece of wood, a piece of carton or a rolled-up newspaper. Carefully apply cotton wool or a thick cloth around the leg. Then apply the splints at the sides of the leg, so that the joints above and under the fracture can no longer move.
- Fasten the splints with tape or bandages, but do not pull them too tight. It is only a matter of immobilising the fracture for the time of transport, so that it does not move.
- Carefully push a blanket or board under the dog and lift the animal up. Make sure that it lies as quietly as possible.
- Take the animal to the veterinarian straight away.

In the case of an open fracture you need to make sure that the animal does not lick or scratch at the fracture. Put plenty of sterile gauze or a clean cloth onto the wound, so that no dirt can get into it. Do not put any salve or iodine onto it, as this only increases the risk of infection. The vet will need to treat an open fracture further.

7. Digestive tract
Vomiting
It is quite normal that dogs sometimes eat grass and throw up. They do this when their stomach bothers them as eating grass stimulates vomiting, which means that the dog discards its stomach contents.

If a dog throws up too often, something is definitely wrong. Throwing up can have different causes, such as infections, worms, eating too much, poisoning and metabolic disturbances. Take your dog to the veterinarian as quickly as possible if it is throwing up heavily, throwing up blood or if it has a swollen belly and a very ill appearance.

If your dog throws up regularly, but does not appear to be unwell generally you can wait and see if the symptoms disappear, feed easily digestible food and consult your vet if necessary. You sometimes need to feed your dog in the evening to prevent so-called 'bile vomiting' in the morning. You can buy special, easily digestible food at your pet shop or veterinarian for such cases. Divide the food into several portions per day, feeding every two to four hours for example, so the stomach gets the ideal opportunity to digest the food. Also make sure that your dog has plenty of fresh drinking water available. When the dog has stopped vomiting completely, you can carefully switch back to normal feeding. Start by replacing ten percent of the diet food with normal food. The next day replace twenty percent, and so on until the diet is one hundred percent normal food. If the problems have not disappeared, you need to contact a vet.

Diarrhoea

When your dog's faeces are soft or watery, it is suffering from diarrhoea. This is a symptom of a disturbed digestion, which can have several causes, such as infection, worms, eating bad or cold food or a sudden change in the diet. If the diarrhoea is bloody, or if it is combined with symptoms such as fever, vomiting and apathy, take your dog to the veterinarian as soon as possible.

If your dog is suffering from light diarrhoea without being ill in any other way, feed it an easily digestible diet to solve the problem. Your vet or pet shop will have special, easily digestible feeds. Divide the feed into several smaller portions per day and feed it until the symptoms disappear, then slowly go back to normal food. This is best done by replacing ten percent of the diet food by normal food daily until the diet is one hundred per cent normal food. Always contact your vet if the diarrhoea persists for more than a day or two.

8. Other injuries
Bruises

To control the swelling, you can cover a bruise with a towel soaked in cold water or with ice cubes wrapped in a towel.

Traffic Accident Trauma

If a dog is hit by a car, immediately contact a vet and make sure that other drivers become aware of the accident by clearly marking the scene. If necessary, hold the dog in a restraining grip, and carefully check if there are any bleeding wounds before treating the dog for shock.

French Bulldog

Carefully cover the dog with a coat or blanket and let it lie quietly until you can get it to a vet. It is very important that you do not move the dog unnecessarily, even if no blood or wounds are visible at first sight, as the dog may have suffered internal injuries. You must also therefore avoid giving the dog anything to drink until it has been examined by a vet.

Footpad injury
If your dog is walking awkwardly or licking its paw, there might be a splinter or another object stuck in the sole of its foot. You can carefully remove this with tweezers, disinfect the spot with iodine straight away and bandage it. This prevents the dog licking at the wound and thus infecting it. In the case of heavy blood loss, or if the object is stuck deep in the sole, you need to take your dog to the veterinarian.

Choking
Dogs like to play with all sorts of things, and it is not uncommon for a dog to swallow something by accident. This can result in different consequences ranging from serious to less acute, depending on the size and shape of the object. In the worst case, the swallowed object is stuck just before the windpipe and the dog can no longer breathe - this is obviously a life-threatening situation. An object, which ends up in the gullet, causes discomfort and sometimes a lot of pain, but the dog is not necessarily in immediate danger. You can recognise when a dog has an object stuck in the gullet by the dog swallowing frequently and trying to throw up. The dog will drool a lot and rub its muzzle. In this case, proceed as follows:

- Hold your dog in a restraining grip if it does not want to accept your help.
- The dog will usually vomit; giving it food or water will only make things worse.
- An object in the gullet is a nuisance, but not life-threatening, therefore remain calm. However, if the object is close to the windpipe, the animal will be in danger, which means that you need to act quickly.
- Open its mouth as far as possible and look into its throat. If the sharp teeth make it difficult to hold the muzzle open, take a dry tissue to carefully pull out the tongue. The dog will keep its mouth open, as it will not risk biting its tongue.
- If the object is clearly visible, you can carefully remove it with tweezers or small pliers. If an object is located just before the windpipe, you can sometimes remove it by putting a finger behind it, deep in the throat. Someone else will have to push on the right spot of the throat from the outside.
- If you do not succeed, lay the dog on its side on a hard surface.
- Apply pressure just behind the last ribs, where the thorax is widest. Push downwards and forwards with both hands, this sometimes makes the object shoot out of the throat.
- Repeat this action several times quickly one after another if you do not succeed the first time. If the object is still stuck in the throat, try removing the object from the throat with your fingers, while someone else continues pressing behind the ribs. If necessary, apply mouth-to-mouth resuscitation.
- If the object has not been removed within a few minutes, take your dog to the veterinarian as quickly as possible. Even if you do manage to remove the object, your vet will still need to examine your dog for possible complications, such as damage to the throat or gullet. Do not take any risks opening the dog's mouth or removing an object - watch your hands and fingers!

Your dog may have swallowed a sharp object, such as a splinter or a fish bone. They will usually get caught in the mucous membranes of the mouth. In this case your dog will rub its muzzle a lot with its paw. It will also salivate excessively, sometimes mixed with blood or retch. Some dogs might sit quietly in one corner, whereas others will run around the house like maniacs.

- Try to have a good look into your dog's throat. If necessary, apply a restraining grip.
- If you have localised the sharp object, you can carefully try to remove it. If it is stuck very tightly, leave it.
- Carefully wipe the froth from the oral cavity and take your dog to the veterinarian as quickly as possible.
- During your journey, hold onto your dog's paws, so that he cannot injure himself by continuously rubbing his muzzle.
- Your vet will remove the object, probably under anaesthetic. After this, your dog will have some problems eating and will need to be fed an adjusted diet.

Wounds

A dog can become wounded in a number of ways. You may therefore encounter a wide range of wounds, which vary in their severity. Roughly, you can divide them into simple wounds, in which only the skin surface has been damaged and complex wounds, in which deeper layers, such as muscles, blood vessels and nerves have also been affected. Both types obviously need to be treated in their own way.

Always take your dog to the veterinarian if it has suffered a severe wound. Graze wounds are best cleaned with warm boiled water.

Modern home hazards

Modern homes are actually a very strange environment for a dog. There are no trees, no grass, and no shrubs and the wind does not blow around their ears. An animal needs to adapt to this domestic setting, and this does not always go smoothly, but you can help make your dog's life with you as safe as possible.

A human walks on two legs and does not always see what can happen at ankle and knee height. You could say that anything that may be dangerous for a crawling baby can also be dangerous for a dog. For example:

Cables
Young dogs like to bite into all sorts of things. Wires from lamps, the computer and other electric appliances can be found everywhere in the house. Hide these where possible, and you can also buy certain materials to wrap around cables to protect them.

Detergents
Although most people do not think of detergents as being immediate hazards for dogs, they contain substances that are toxic. So it stands to reason that you should not let your dog come into contact with detergents. Therefore, it is important to be aware that your dog can ingest toxins from his paws after you have mopped the floor, for example, so exercise extreme caution when using any household cleaning products.

Chocolate
Chocolate is one of those products that humans enjoy, but which is actually toxic for dogs. It contains certain substances that their bodies cannot break down, so never feed a dog chocolate and make sure it isn't left around where your French Bulldog can find it.

Avocado
Avocado is also toxic for dogs. It contains persine, which causes serious conditions in dogs.

Onions and garlic
Avoid onions and also garlic, both raw as well as cooked for dogs. It contains a substance that can cause anemia in dogs.

Grapes and raisins
Grapes and raisins are also prohibited for dogs. 30 grams per kilogram of bodyweight is considered toxic and can lead to kidney failure.

Plants
t is common knowledge that dogs sometimes like to eat grass and this, generally, is nothing to be concerned about.
You never know why a dog will take a fancy to a plant, and puppies in particular occasionally like to 'take a bite'. In reality it is unlikely your dog will actually eat a house-plant, but if it does happen, take your dog and a branch of the plant in question to your vet, they will know the best course of action.
On the next pages an overview of toxic home and garden plants is provided.

TOXIC PLANTS

-A-

Abrus precatorius	- Precatory-pea
Acer rubrum	- Red maple
Aconitum napellus	- Monk's hood
Aesculus hippocastanum	- Horse chestnut
Ailanthus altissima	- Tree-of-heaven
Allamanda cathartica	- Golden-trumper
Allium cepa	- Onion
Allium sativum	- Garlic
Alstroemeria ligtu	- Peruvian lily
Amaranthus hybridus	- Smooth pigweed
Amaryllis vittata	- Amaryllis *(A. vittata)*
Anthurium andraenum	- Flamingo lily
Aquilegia alpina	- Aquilegia
Asimina triloba	- Pawpaw

Aquilegia

-B-

Baptista tinctoria	- Wild indigo
Barbarea vulgaris	- Yellow rocket
Buxus sempervirens	- Buxus

Buxus

-C-

Caladium bicolor	- Caladium
Chrysanthemum indicum	- Chrysanthemum
Cicuta virosa	- Northern water-hemlock
Clematis	- Clematis
Clivia miniata	- Kaffir lily
Codiaeum variegetum	- Croton
Colchicum autumnale	- Autumn crocus
Conium macaltum	- Poison-hemlock
Convallaria majalis	- Lily-of-the-valley
Corydalis	- Corydalis
Crocus	- Crocus
Cyclamen persicum	- Cyclamen

Clematis

-D-

Dature innoxia	- Angel's trumpet
Datura stramonium	- Jimsomweed
Delphinium	- Larkspur
Dieffenbachia seguine	- Mother-in-law-plant
Digitalis purpurea	- Foxglove

Corydalis

-E-

Euonymus europaeus	- European spindletree
Euphorbia helioscopia	- Sun spurge
Euphorbia lacteal	- Candelabra-cactus
Euphorbia pulcherrima	- Poinsettia

Crocus

-F-

Fagopyrum esculentem	- Tall manna grass

-G-

Gutierrezia sarothrae	- Broom snakewood
Gymnocladus dioicus	- Kentucky coffeetree

-H-

Hedera helix	- English ivy
Helenium autumnale	- Sneezeweed
Helianthus annuus	- Sunflower
Heliotropium curassavicum	- Spatulate-leaved heliotrope
Heracleum mantegazzianum	- Giant hogweed
Humulus lupulus	- Common hop
Hyancinthoides nonscripta	- English bluebell
Hydrangea macrophylla	- Hydrangea
Hypercum perforatum	- St. John's wort

-I-

Ilex aquifolium	- English holly
Ipomoea tricolour	- Morning glory
Iris pseudocorus	- Yellow iris
Iris versicolor	- Blue flag iris

-J-

Juglans nigra	- Black walnut

-K-

Kalanchoe daigremontiana	- Devil's-backbone
Kalmia angustofolia	- Sheep-laurel

-L-

Laportea canadensus	- Canada nettle
Lathyrus odoratus	- Sweet pea
Lathyrus sativus	- Grass pea
Leonurus cardiaca	- Motherwort
Ligistrum vulgare	- Common privet
Linaria vulgaris	- Yellow toadflax
Lobelia cardinalis	- Cardinalflower
Lobelia inflate	- Indian-tobacco
Lonicera xylosteum	- Fly honeysuckle
Lupinus argenteus	- Silvery lupine
Lupinus polyphyllus	- Large-leaved lupine
Lupinus pusillus	- Small lupine
Lupinus sericeus	- Silky lupine

-M-

Mangifera indica	- Mango
Medicago sativa	- Alfalfa
Melilotus alba	- White sweet clover
Melitus officinalis	- Yellow sweet clover
Menispermum canadense	- Moonseed
Monstera deliciosa	- Swiss-cheese plant

-N-

Narcissus peoticus	- Narcissus
Narcissus pseudonarcissus	- Daffodil

Delphinium

Datura   Digitalis

Euonymus

Hedera   Hydrangea

Ilex   Lonicera

| *Nerium oleander* | - Oleander |
| *Nicotiana tabacum* | - Tobacco |

-O-

Onoclea sensibilis	- Sensitive fern
Ornithogalum umbellatum	- Star-of-Bethlehem
Oxytropus lambertii	- Purple locoweed

-P-

Papaver nudicaule	- Iceland poppy
Papaver orientale	- Oriental poppy
Papaver somniferum	- Opium poppy
Parthenocissus quinquefolia	- Virginia creeper
Persea americana	- Avocado
Phacelia campanularia	- California canarygrass
Phalaris arundinacea	- Reed canarygrass
Philodendron cordatum	- Philodendron
Phoradendron flavescens	- American mistletoe
Physalis alkekengi	- Chinese-lantern
Physalis peruviana	- Ground-cherry
Phytolacca american	- Pokeweed
Pinus ponderosa	- Ponderosa pine
Primula obconica	- Primula
Polygonatum multiflorum	- Solomon's seal
Prunus pennsylvanica	- Pin cherry
Ptedidium aquilinum	- Bracken

-Q-

| *Quercus alba* | - White oak |
| *Quercus rubra* | - Red oak |

-R-

Rananculus bulbosus	- Bulbous buttercup
Raphanus raphanistrum	- Wild radish
Raphanus sativus	- Radish
Rhamnus carthartica	- European buckthorn
Rheum rhaponticum	- Rhubarb
Rhododendron macrophyllum	- California rose-baby
Rhus diversiloba	- Western poison-oak
Rhus radicans	- Poison ivy
Ricinus communis	- Castor-bean
Robinia pseudoacacia	- Black locust
Rudbeckia serotina	- Black-eyed Susan
Rumex acetosa	- Garden sorrel

-S-

Sambucus canadensis	- American elder
Sambucus nigra	- European elder
Sarcobatus vermiculatus	- Greasewood
Scilla siberica	- Siberian scilla
Senecop jacobaea	- Tansy ragwort
Sinapis arvensis	- Wild mustard
Solanum dulcamara	- Climbing nightshade
Solanum nigrum	- Black nightshade
Solanum speudocapsicum	- Jerusalem-cherry

Lupinus

Papaver orientalis

Parthenocissus

Phytolacca

Polygonatum   Rhododendron

Solanum tuberosum	- Potato
Solidago mollis	- Velvety goldenrod
Sorghum halepense	- Johnson grass
Suckleya suckleyana	- Poison suckleya
Symphoricarpos albus	- Thin-leaved snowberry
Symphytum asperum	- Prickly comfrey
Symplocarpus foetidus	- Skunk cabbage

Ricinus

-T-

Tanacetum vulgare	- Tansy
Taxus canadensis	- Canada yew
Thermopsis rhombifolia	- Golden-bean
Thlaspi arvense	- Stinkweed
Thuja	- Thuja
Trifolium pratense	- Red clover
Trifolium repens	- White clover
Tulipa gesneriana	- Tulip

-U-

| *Urica dioica* | - Stinging nettle |

Sedum spectabile

-V-

Veratrum viride	- False hellebore
Viburnum opulus	- Guelder-rose
Vicia sativa	- Common vetch

-W-

| *Wisteria floribunda* | - Japanese wisteria |

-X-

| *Xanthium strumarium* | - Cocklebur |

-Z-

| *Zigadenus elegans* | - White camas |

Thuja

Tips

- Get in touch with a breed club for the address of a reliable breeder.
- Visit more than one breeder before buying a puppy.
- Ask to see the parent dogs' papers. The parents must not have any hereditary abnormalities. Ask to see the health checks that are made.
- Never buy a puppy if you have been unable to see its mother.
- Never buy a French Bulldog on impulse.
- The first trip in a car is a real experience for a puppy; make it a pleasant one.
- Do not add supplements to ready-made foods.
- Do not let your French Bulldog climb up stairs for the first six months.
- Join a puppy-training course with your puppy. It teaches both dog and owner a lot.
- Take care that your dog does not get overweight. An appropriate diet and plenty of exercise are golden rules.
- Never leave a dog alone with small children.
- Never let your puppy run endlessly after a ball.
- Do not just fight the fleas, but the larvae too.
- Organise a holiday home or a dog-sitter for your French Bulldog well in advance.
- Think carefully before you decide to take your dog on holiday - it may not be the best option for the dog!
- Allow your French Bulldog to rest after meals.
- A puppy will mean a lot of work, and sometimes a few grey hairs.
- Good grooming is important for your dog's health.
- Early training is essential to ensure you end up with a well-behaved dog.
- Let your French Bulldog NEVER GET OVERHEATED AND STRESSED OR OVER ACTIVATED IN HOT WEATHER! It can kill the dog!

Internet

A great deal of information can be found on the internet. A selection of websites with interesting details and links to other sites and pages are listed here. Sometimes pages move to another site or address. You can find more sites by using the available search engines.

For Great Britain

www.frenchbulldogclubofengland.org.uk
The French Bulldog Club of England was founded in 1902 by a small group of enthusiast French Bulldog lovers.
Their aim was and still is the preservation, promotion, and well being of the breed. After a history of more than 100 years those aims remain unchanged.

www.mncfrenchbulldogclub.co.uk/
The Midland & Northern Counties French Bulldog Club was granted official status by the Kennel Club on November 11th 1958. Their aim was to have another breed club to cater specifically for those who lived in the Midlands and the North. The parent club, The French Bulldog Club of England, held most of its functions in and around London.

Dog-related websites

www.thekennelclub.org.uk
The British Kennel Club's primary objective is to promote, in every way, the general improvement of dogs. This site aims to provide you with information you may need to be a responsible pet owner and to help you keep your dog happy, safe and content.

www.k9-care.co.uk
The Self-Help site for dog owners. A beautiful website with tons of information on dogs. All you need to know about grooming, training, health care, buying a dog, travel and much more.

www.doggenetichealth.org
Your one stop resource for practical information and to learn about dog genetic health. A guide for dog breeders and owners, brought to you by The Kennel Club.

www.thedogscene.co.uk
This website is run by dog lovers for dog lovers in the UK. Their primary purpose is to spread the word about responsible dog ownership and dog breeding. They provide you with all the help and information and the right contacts that you need to have a happy, healthy relationship with your dog. The Dog Scene provides a lot of information concerning dogs, and more is being added all the time.

For U.S.A.

www.akc.org
The website of the American Kennel Club, with lots and lots of information.

www.ukcdogs.com/
The website of the United Kennel Club, this club was established in 1998. It is the largest all-breed performance-dog registry in the world, registering dogs from all 50 states and 25 foreign countries.

www.frenchbulldogclub.org/
The French Bulldog Club of America, was founded in 1897. The F.B.D.C.A. is the oldest French Bulldog Club in the world. Their aim is to help people who are interested in all aspects of the French Bulldog, such as competing in conformation and performance events, breeding, judging, and just owning and loving their dogs.
Great site with lots of information any breeder and owner should know.

www.frenchbulldogrescue.org/
French Bulldog Rescue Network. The French Bulldogs come into the F.B.R.N. from various sources. That can be from commercial breeding kennels, import-brokers, public shelters, private rescue groups or even Good Samaritans who try to save the lives of dogs. However most of the dogs in the French Bulldog Rescue Network are French Bulldogs that are turned over by their owners, because they can no longer keep them. The French Bulldog Rescue Network is there to help all these poor French Bulldogs.
The F.B.R.N. is a volunteer organisation and is funded entirely by contributions.
Maybe you can find your French Bulldog through this organisation.

www.aboutpets.info
The website of the publisher of the About Pets book series. An overview of the titles, availability in which languages and where in the world the books are sold.

Addresses

Becoming a member of a breed club can be very useful for good advice and interesting activities. A French Bulldog club will give you the opportunity to meet other French Bulldog lovers. Contact The Kennel Club in case addresses or telephone numbers have changed.

For Great Brittain

The Kennel Club
1 – 5 Clarges Street
Piccadilly
London WIJ 8AB
Tel.: 0870 606 6750
Fax: 020 7518 1058
www.thekennelclub.org.uk

Scottish Kennel Club
Eskmills Park Station Road Musselburgh
Edinburgh EH21 7PQ
Tel.: 0131 665 3920
Fax: 0131 653 6937
www.scottishkennelclub.org
E-mail: info@scottishkennelclub.org

The Irish Kennel Club LTD
Fottrell House
Harolds X Bridge,
Dublin 6W
Ireland
Tel.: +353 (1) 4533 300 - 4532 309 - 4532 310
Fax: +353 (1) 4533 237
www.ikc.ie
E-mail: ikenclub@indigo.ie

The French Bulldog Club of England
www.frenchbulldogclubofengland.org.uk
E-mail: honsecfbce@aol.com

The Midland & Northern Counties French Bulldog Club
www.mncfrenchbulldogclub.co.uk/
E-mail: jmm@sky.com

For U.S.A.

American Kennel Club
AKC Customer Care
8051 Arco Corporate Drive, Suite 100
Raleigh, NC 27617-3390
Tel.: 00 1 919 233 9767 from 08:30 until 17.00 o'clock
weekdays (Monday - Friday) except holidays
www.akc.org

UKC
100 E Kilgore Rd Kalamazoo
MI 49002 – 5584
Office hours: 09:00 to 16:30 (E.S.T.)
Monday through Friday
Tel.: 269 - 343 - 9020
Fax: 269 - 343 - 7037
www.ukcdogs.com/

Breed Association

The French Bulldog Club of America
ww.frenchbulldogclub.org/
E-mail secr.: pkosinar@sunflower.com

French Bulldog Rescue Network
www.frenchbulldogrescue.org/
E-mail: webmaster@frenchbulldogrescue.org

Profile

Name:	French Bulldog
Original name:	Bouledogue Français
Origin:	France
Breed group:	U.K. Kennel Club: Utility Group A.K.C.: Non Sporting Group
F.C.I. Classification:	Group 9 - Companion and Toy Dogs Section 11- Small Molossian Dogs without working trial
Breed Association established:	In France Marcel Roger founded the breeding club in 1888, and 1898, the breed was also accepted by the Société Centrale Canine of France and officially recognised as a breed. The French Bulldog Club of America was founded in 1897. In Great Britain the French Bulldog Club was established in 1902.
First breed standard:	In France the first breed standard was drawn up in 1888.
Original use:	Ratter and lap dog.
Use today:	Companion dog and lap dog.
Weight:	Bitch: 11 kg (24 lbs) Dog: 12,5 kg (28 lbs)
Life expectancy (average):	13 to 14 years